Make Your Money Last Forever

Make Your *Money* Last Forever

How to Maximize Your Potential for Creating Eternal Wealth

JULAINE SMITH

∞ ETERNAL WEALTH
PUBLICATIONS

Unless otherwise noted, Scripture references are from the Holy Bible, New International Version®. Copyright © 1973, 1978, 1984 International Bible Society. Used by permission of Zondervan. All rights reserved.

Scripture quotations marked KJV are taken from the King James Version.

Scripture quotations marked NKJV are taken from the Holy Bible, New King James Version. Copyright © 1982 by Thomas Nelson, Inc. Used by permission. All rights reserved.

Scripture quotations marked NLT are taken from the Holy Bible, New Living Translation, copyright © 1996. Used by permission of Tyndale House Publishers, Inc., Wheaton, Illinois 60189. All rights reserved.

This publication is designed to provide accurate and authoritative information in regard to the subject matter covered. It is published with the understanding that the publisher and author are not engaged in rendering legal, accounting, or other professional service. If legal advice or other professional advice, including financial, is required, the services of a competent professional person should be sought.

Eternal Wealth Publications
4957 Lakemont Blvd SE, Suite C-4 #201
Bellevue, WA 98006

Copyright © 2007 by Julaine Smith

All rights reserved. No part of this book may be reproduced or transmitted in any form or by any means, electronic or mechanical, including photocopying, recording or by any information storage and retrieval system, without written permission from the author, except for inclusion of brief quotations in a review.

Library of Congress Control Number: 2006905913
Smith, Julaine.
   Make your money last forever: how to maximize your potential for creating eternal wealth / Julaine Smith
   p.cm.

ISBN 0-9779480-0-5
ISBN 978-0-9779480-0-0

*To my husband, Terence, and son, Jonathan,
into whom I will always remember to pour my love*

Contents

Acknowledgments ix
Introduction 1

Part 1. Understanding Eternal Wealth

1. Loving God and Making Money 11
   We were made to prosper.

2. Principles of Eternal Wealth 29
   Take up the seven keys to building wealth in God's kingdom.

3. God's Family Enterprise 51
   Taking care of the Lord's family is God's top priority.

4. God's Enterprise in the World 65
   Our money has a mission.

5. The Entanglement of Worldly Wealth 79
   Beware of the danger of prosperity and Babylon's seduction.

6. The Invisible Hand 95
   God has a guide to eternal wealth.

Part 2. Creating Eternal Wealth

7. Discovering Your Purpose for Eternal Wealth 109
   You can have an eternal purpose for your prosperity.

8. The Essentials of Soul Prosperity 133
   As our soul prospers, we prosper.

9. The American Dream Revisited 157
   Of the one to whom much is given much is required.

10. Purposeful and Profitable Action 173
    Your career is your marketplace ministry.

11. Strategically Managing Financial Resources.............. 201
    You can use worldly wealth to make kingdom friends.

12. Building Relationships and Strategic Alliances............ 221
    God's going to get the glory out of this.

Notes 233
Recommended Reading................................... 237
About the Author 239

Acknowledgments

Having spent many years working on this book project, I have had the privilege of working with lots of people along the way.

Thank you, Ron Worman, for seeing something in me long before I could perceive it and then helping me discover what it was.

Thanks also to my spiritual parents, Pastor Wendell and Virginia Smith. You model giving with such perfection and teach the purpose for prosperity with such grace that every member of The City Church can't help but be impacted by your lives and want to prosper…God's way. Thank you for teaching me how to walk humbly and to use my gifts unselfishly.

Thanks to my literary team: Ed Stewart, Elisa Stanford, Eric Stanford, Rose Yancik, and Laura Barker. There wouldn't be a book if it weren't for your skill with words and publishing. Thank you for showing me how to take what was in my heart, translate it into words and present it to the world.

Thank you, Rhonda Bremond, Susan Camerer, Mattie George, Debbie Hill, Anita Johnson, Carley McLaughlin, Dr. Mary Miller, Jan Rodgers, Tracy Solomon, and Pat Sween. You are my girlfriends, the women of God who encouraged me along the way, prayed with me, and wouldn't let me give up on my dream. Thank you all so much for your powerful prayers!

Thank you, Mom and Dad, Lawrence and Vivian Givens, for raising me in an environment where love, hard work, and shooting for the stars, even if you miss and hit the moon, were esteemed values. You taught me to never give up the Lion of the Tribe of Judah's fight, and for that I'm eternally grateful.

Thanks to my sister, the Rev. Dr. Diane Givens Moffett, and her daughter, the Rev. Eustacia Marshall, for challenging me to explore theological writings beyond what I otherwise would have ventured to read. Our Presbyterian heritage is the foundation upon which my faith is built. Thanks for fanning the flames and keeping me grounded.

Thanks to my ancestors, upon whose shoulders I stand. The entrepreneurial spirit that flows through my veins was first birthed in you. You owned the land, the laundry service, and the stores. It is because of your hard work and sacrifice that I am able to stand.

A well-known praise song says, "God saves the best for last." It's in that spirit that I must acknowledge and thank my husband, Terence, who from the beginning of our marriage encouraged me to work in the marketplace. Honey, you must have somehow known that it was my destiny. Thank you for pushing me, supporting me, being patient with me, and most of all, believing in me. I love you…totally.

> When you get to the finish line
>
> of the race we call life,
>
> will you have run the right race?

Introduction

A runner awoke on the morning of the New York Marathon with a sense of excitement and confidence about the day's race. After a light breakfast, it was time for her to begin the two-hour drive from her home in Connecticut to the starting line in Manhattan. As she pulled onto the turnpike, panic struck as she realized that she had left the directions to the starting line on the breakfast table.

She realized that she didn't have enough time to go back home and get the directions. But she had a vague idea about where the race was going to start and reasoned that she'd be able to ask for directions if she got lost. So she kept driving.

After a few wrong turns, she approached the area where she believed the event was to take place, and there, to her relief, she saw signs and colorful flags marking the registration area for runners. Looking at her watch, she saw that, with the time she had spent driving around, she now would have to dash to the registration table if she was going to make it there before the race started.

Properly registered, the runner made her way toward the starting line just before the gun went off, signaling the beginning of the race. Though she started near the back of the pack, she maneuvered through the other runners relatively easily and was soon leading the race. She had trained hard and was expecting to run a good race, but still she was surprised by how easy it was to leave the other runners behind her. She set a good pace and led for the rest of the course.

After securing an easy victory, she walked proudly to the winners' table to claim her prize. She began to realize something was wrong when she was handed a small trophy and no prize money.

"Wait a minute," she exclaimed to the man announcing her name as the winner. "This is the wrong prize. I was expecting five thousand dollars plus a much nicer trophy than this."

"Oh, you were?" he responded. "That sounds like the prize for the winner of the New York Marathon."

"Yes," she replied. "That's the race I just won!"

"Oh no," he responded. "That race is still in progress. Those runners started about ten minutes after this race, and their starting line was two blocks east of here. The race you won was the race for beginning runners."

When I started my career as a certified public accountant in 1987, it was the beginning of a race that I had spent many years preparing to run. Since I was a young girl, around six years of age, I had desired to do one thing in life: make lots of money. I'd had a few starts and stops along the way, but finally I had made my way to work I knew would turn all my dreams for financial success into reality.

As I began my CPA career, I was proud of my accomplishments and confident in my abilities. My confidence was partly due to my successful academic career and partly a result of knowing that God was walking with me on this journey. You see, my career as a CPA started as a consequence of my making the decision to give my life 100 percent to Jesus Christ and then hearing God tell me to go back to school and become an accountant. So I just knew God was okay with what I was about to do.

At the time I wasn't concerned about whether I would be able to live a life of obedience to God while prospering financially. The thought that I might get to a point where I was trying to love God while serving money never entered my mind. I had no concerns about financial wealth causing me to become prideful or arrogant toward God, since God and I were so close. He was orchestrating the events of my life, and I was going along with what I was sure was going to be a fun and financially rewarding ride.[1]

The only concern I had was my lack of understanding about how my desire to be a successful businesswoman fit in with the Great Commission. I felt my contribution to God's ministry was limited by the fact that I didn't spend most of my hours at church doing ministry. I believed that, even though I was following God's plan for my life, somehow that plan wasn't as important as, say, pastoring a church or working on the mission field. In the end I decided just to do the best I could at my work in accounting.

Then, during the financial heyday of the 1990s, I began to listen to a televangelist preach a message that I have since learned is referred to as the *prosperity gospel*. This preacher was saying that God wants his people to prosper financially, that wealth is a sign of his blessing. In all my years of going to church, I had never heard such a thing. But now that I had heard it, I was elated!

By this time in my career, I was beginning to see the full extent of my earning potential—and it was great. So learning about the prosperity gospel seemed like my Get Out of Jail Free card. It freed me from the guilt I had about wanting to make a lot of money and spending my working hours in the marketplace instead of the church. It also raised the sense of value I associated with the job I was doing, because preachers were acknowledging the importance of work. In short, the prosperity gospel gave me the fuel I needed to continue to run the race toward financial wealth.

One fateful day everything changed. I heard God telling me to quit my job and stay home to focus on my family instead. No more big paychecks. No more expanding an already expansive lifestyle. Now what was I going to do?

When I heard this new direction God wanted me to go in, I forecasted the impact on my financial security, concluded that the change in direction was a threat to that security, and decided not to follow God's direction. This change just didn't make sense to me. The same Jesus who had told me to become a CPA, the same Jesus who was blessing me tremendously through my work, the same Jesus who was the author of my success was now threatening that success. I didn't like it one bit. So I chose to disobey his command.

What a mistake! It was a mistake I would take years to recover from. But the fruits of my returning to obedience and relearning what God thinks about money appear on the pages of this book. I believe the insights God gave me through the process I have undergone can help many.

When we choose to run the race of life by following our own rules and forsake the commands of God, we might win great financial wealth, but we will be running the wrong race and at the end of that race we will receive an undesirable prize. The race God calls us to run is not one whose prize is winning great amounts of money, power, and prestige. The race God calls us to run is one in which we pursue the prize of our high calling in Christ Jesus. And running the wrong race results in leaving undone the things God wants us to do and has prepared us to do.

- Are you worried that you might be running the wrong race?
- Are you uncertain about God's purpose for your life and financial prosperity?
- Are you concerned about whether you can prosper financially while living a life of obedience to God?
- Are you afraid that your pursuit of financial wealth may cause you to become proud or arrogant and in doing so miss the call God has on your life?
- Do you have questions about how your desire to be a successful businessperson can fit into the bigger scheme of God's kingdom?
- Do you feel less valued by God than people whom he has called into pastoral ministry?
- Are you confused by the different perspectives on wealth taught throughout the church and looking for a balanced understanding of God's promise?

I promote neither the prosperity gospel nor an antiprosperity message. I want to share with you a fresh biblical look at people, their relationship with money, and the meaning of true wealth. I share these insights from my experience as a certified public accountant, a veteran of corporate finance, an entrepreneur, and a businesswoman. More important, I share from my heart where God, by his Word and his Spirit, is graciously teaching me how people at all economic strata should view their financial and material resources.

The principles I present in this book will help you acquire and manage what I call *eternal wealth*—wealth created God's way. Here's the core of what I want to share with you:

> God stands ready and willing to help you realize your full potential for creating and managing material and financial resources sufficient to meet your needs and the needs of others, advance the kingdom of God in the world, and establish your eternal dwelling place in heaven.

Let me highlight a few important items from this core statement.

First, God wants you to prosper in all areas of your life, including your finances, because prosperity birthed from an intimate relationship with Christ is a reflection of God's empowerment in our lives. Jesus Christ declares, "I am the vine; you are the branches. If a man remains in me and I in him, he will bear much fruit; apart from me you can do nothing" (John 15:5). As with everything else in a believer's life, Jesus is our source, our strength, and our supply for acquiring and managing eternal wealth. We can't do anything without the Lord, and that includes maximizing our potential for creating and managing material and financial resources.

Second, you are integrally involved with God in the process of creating eternal wealth. God will equip you for acquiring eternal wealth, but he's not going to do it for you. Paul instructed, "Continue to work out your salvation with fear and trembling, for it is God who works in you to will and to act according to his good purpose" (Philippians 2:12-13). I've heard it said this way: we are to work out what God works in. God has given us the resources, the tools, and the enabling for eternal wealth, but nothing will happen unless we act in line with his plan for our lives and his purposes for our resources.

Third, eternal wealth involves your money and material possessions, but it goes far beyond that, just as heaven and eternity supersede earth and time. Jesus said, "A person's life does not consist in the abundance of his possessions" (Luke 12:15). Paul wrote, "We brought nothing into the world, and we can take nothing out of it" (1 Timothy 6:7). The richest people in the world will enjoy their wealth only for a lifetime. As someone has quipped, you never see a hearse pulling a U-Haul trailer, reminding us that we can't take it with us. But we can send it ahead of us. Whatever money and material possessions we invest in God's purposes in this life—out of our love for, obedience to, and relationship with God—will pay dividends for eternity.

> God stands ready and willing to help you realize your full potential for creating and managing material and financial resources sufficient to meet your needs and the needs of others, advance the kingdom of God in the world, and establish your eternal dwelling place in heaven.

Fourth, you are to be a channel, not a reservoir, for eternal wealth. Jesus is on a mission in this world, and people are at the center of his mission. He loves people and is out to rescue them from a life of sin that leads to destruction. And since Jesus is our Lord, his mission is automatically our mission. That means our wealth has a mission that is God-determined, not self-determined. The assumption that the material resources God equips us to acquire and manage are primarily for our benefit reflects a gross misunderstanding of the purpose of wealth. Everything belongs to God, and he has every right to reprioritize our lives and redistribute what we have in order to further his mission of love. Any claim of ownership on our part is nothing short of selfish, shortsighted arrogance.

This book is your doorway into eternal wealth. As you read these pages, your view of how a person acquires, enjoys, uses, and relates to money will be transformed. And I promise that if you implement the principles I share, you will start seeing a difference in your "bottom line." Not only will you be encouraged to discover God's purpose for your prosperity and to always obey his direction regarding your career, but you will also discover fresh, God-centered motivation for maximizing your earning potential and managing the resources he puts into your hands.

Best of all, you will experience the joy of knowing that the dividends of your stewardship under God's direction will last forever in the form of the lives you touch and the rewards you accrue "where moth and rust do not destroy, and where thieves do not break in and steal" (Matthew 6:20). When you get to the finish line of the race we call life, you will receive your just reward for the work you've done because you will have run the right race.

So let's get started on your bottom line. In part 1 we will fully explore eternal wealth—what it is, what it's for, and what its primary rival for our allegiance in this life is: worldly wealth. And in part 2 we will delve into the principles and strategies for acquiring and managing eternal wealth.

PART

1

Understanding Eternal Wealth

" God isn't anxious about his people being rich. "

Chapter 1

Loving God and Making Money

On Sunday morning at one urban church the time comes to pass the offering plates. The church members silently hope the pastor doesn't bring up any special needs of the church, such as the building maintenance that needs attending to. *Money shouldn't be spent on something as temporal as the church building,* they think. *It's okay if the church building looks lived in; after all, my house does.* In fact, some churchgoers don't want to hear about money at church, period. *Please don't mention the word "tithe,"* they inwardly moan. *No one wants to be made to feel guilty about giving less than ten percent of their income to the church.* Others think, *God never intended for us to go without so that the church could have more,* or *These preachers are just trying to line their own pockets.* As the offering plate is passed down their pew, members begin to relax because once again the pastor has tastefully decided not to talk about money and they were able to give their meager offering quickly and painlessly…and without conviction.

Meanwhile, at the church down the street the experience is different. The preacher makes the announcement thunderously: "It's offering time!"

The congregation explodes in excitement and cheers. Most of the members can't wait for offering time. They especially enjoy it when they can join in the parade of givers by bringing their offering up front and placing it in the plates held by deacons or elders. For them, offering is a joyous and celebrated time of worship, full of music, shouts of joy, and expressions of adoration toward God. And the testimonies about God's financial blessings are so encouraging! One person shares about how he was able to buy a new house with no money down and bad credit. Another exults in the promotion she just received. "We give and God gives it back to us," the pastor proclaims, responding with joy for the outpouring of God's blessing on his church. A visitor sits in silent amazement, wondering, *Is this place for real?*

It *is* for real. *Both* churches are for real. I know—I have attended both. And perhaps you have been a member of churches much like them. But my purpose in describing these two divergent offering times is to illustrate how much disagreement there is among Christians over the subject of money. How much wealth and how many material possessions does God want us to have? And how does he want us to give them to his work?

Most Christians admit that the earth is the Lord's and that everything in it belongs to him (see Psalm 24:1). They agree that all we have ultimately was given to us by God and belongs to God. But there is a lot of talk and disagreement these days about prosperity and the role money should or shouldn't play in a believer's life. Churches don't agree on how to interpret the full counsel of Scripture as it pertains to the subject of money and whether God wants his disciples to be rich.

Some people take Deuteronomy 8:18 ("God…gives you the ability to produce wealth") literally; some people don't. But I didn't write this book to debate the prosperity message. I wrote it because I believe people are looking for answers to their questions about money and they are confused by the conflicting teachings on the doctrine of giving.

Further, I wrote it because I believe some people are held captive by the world's system designed to produce wealth even as they think they are on God's pathway to wealth. The world's preoccupation with material prosperity, "bling-bling," and luxurious lifestyles has infiltrated more than a few churches. But there is a difference between, on the one hand, living a prosperous life as a result of keeping God's commandments and, on the other hand, obtaining wealth and riches through disobeying God's Word.

My hope is that, after reading this book, you will understand the difference between the pathway to creating wealth God's way—something I call *eternal wealth*—and the pathway to creating wealth the world's way and that you'll assess for yourself which pathway you're on. If you determine that you've ventured off course, I hope you will begin to transform your thinking about money and tap into God's wealth-producing power his way.

I'm going to share with you how I let myself become sidetracked and how God got me back on course to produce wealth with everlasting benefits for my life and his kingdom. But before I begin sharing my story, let's consider responses to this question: how much of what belongs to God are we allowed to acquire for ourselves, and how much should we give back to God through gifts to the church and to the poor and needy? In other words, is there a point of sufficiency when it comes to money—a point where we should say that what we have is enough?

I hear two general but opposite responses to this question. Some people are convinced that God intends them to be poor. Others contend that God wants them to be rich. Let's look at these two views and find out where they came from.

Blessed Are the Poor

As a child growing up in Sunday school, I was taught a couple of things about Jesus that formed my earliest opinion of money. I learned that God wanted me to be like Jesus, and I also learned that Jesus was poor. The Savior of the world was born into a peasant family, I was told. At Jesus' dedication his parents offered a sacrifice of two turtledoves, which was what a family was allowed to give instead of a lamb if they were poor. Even as an adult, Jesus said he had no home of his own (see Matthew 8:20). I understood that the goal of every good churchgoing girl and boy was to be like Jesus. It wasn't difficult for me to connect these ideas and reason that God wanted me to be poor like Jesus.

The Bible stories I heard left me believing that the poor were God's favorites. I learned from the Sermon on the Mount that the poor are blessed, for "theirs is the kingdom of heaven." I took that to mean that since we will be rich in heaven, God wants us to be poor here on earth. Somehow I missed the part of the verse that states "poor in spirit," not just "poor" (Matthew 5:3).

Furthermore, it was apparent to me as a little girl that God didn't like rich people very much. I remember the Bible story about how it's easier for a camel to go through the eye of a needle than for rich people to enter God's kingdom (see Matthew 19:24). I knew how big a camel was and how small a needle's eye was. So I concluded that if I was going to make it into heaven, I'd better be poor, not rich. Many Christians today have come to similar conclusions from what they have been taught or what they have read in the Bible.

There are shades of difference in how people live out this conviction, from thinking that wealth is at best a distraction to a Christian's life of sacrificial obedience to thinking that having wealth is at worst a sin. Here are some of the "biblical proofs" people sometimes offer for why they should live with less rather than more.

1. Money is evil.

One of the most frequently misquoted verses in the Bible by Christians and non-Christians alike is 1 Timothy 6:10. You hear people spout, "Money is the root of all evil" and insist that the less money we have, the more righteous we can become. In reality the verse states, "The *love* of money is a root of all kinds of evil" (emphasis added).

Luke 16:13 is another verse that is used to support the evils of money: "You cannot serve both God and Money." Some people interpret this verse to mean that God and money are polar opposites, like good and evil or heaven and hell. If God is on one side, then whatever is in opposition to him—in this case money—must certainly be evil and anti-God.

But if you notice, we're not challenged to choose between God and money but between serving God and serving money, which Jesus taught were direct opposites.

2. "Deny yourself" money and nice things.

Jesus said, "If anyone would come after me, he must deny himself and take up his cross and follow me" (Matthew 16:24). Some people derive from this call to discipleship the idea that Jesus doesn't want his followers to have (much less enjoy) wealth and nice things. They point to the apostles, who "left everything and followed him" (Luke 5:9-11, 27-28; see also Matthew 19:27). Any attachment to the material world impedes our journey with Christ. But Jesus is not saying we shouldn't have or enjoy wealth or nice things. He is saying that our allegiance must always be to doing God's will, even if it means giving away everything we have.

3. It's a sin to be rich.

A religious and rich young man came to Jesus, asking how to gain eternal life. After a discussion of the man's genuinely good and righteous behavior, Jesus said to him, "If you want to be perfect, go, sell your possessions and give to the poor, and you will have treasure in heaven. Then come, follow me" (Matthew 19:21). What was keeping this fine young gentleman from treasure in heaven? Apparently it was his money. So Jesus told him to give it all away. Some people interpret this encounter to mean that wealth automatically blocks our relationship with God. And for some people that may be true. But once again, Jesus wasn't establishing that as an absolute truth for all people. Instead he was demonstrating that when our hearts belong to things instead of to God, then our possessions will block our ability to follow God. The question every person must answer is whether they love God more than money.

4. *The poorer you are, the better.*
Jesus took his disciples to the temple treasury for a lesson on money. He watched many rich people donate substantial cash offerings, but he reserved his words of praise for a poor widow who put in her last two copper coins: "I tell you the truth, this poor widow has put more into the treasury than all the others. They all gave out of their wealth; but she, out of her poverty, put in everything—all she had to live on" (Mark 12:43-44). Does this scene suggest to you that being poor is a high virtue? Some people see it that way when in fact Jesus was saying that when any person, rich or poor, is willing to give everything they have to God because of their love and devotion to him, that is a high virtue.

People with a God-wants-us-poor mentality find it difficult to spend money on frills or luxuries for themselves. Some even choose not to earn more or extra money because of the temptation to overabundance and the fear of "crossing the line," since they don't know where God's "boundary" for wealth is. They allow their fear of overabundance to drive them to live as thriftily as possible in order to avoid any appearance of loving money and to ensure that they will never acquire too much in this life.

For example, some people view buying a new car as excessive and wasteful, since a reliable used car is much less expensive. And they would never consider buying a luxury car of any vintage. To save money, they shun name brands for generic brands whenever possible. And they feel guilty buying anything that isn't on sale or closeout.

There is certainly nothing wrong with living frugally and even sacrificially in order to give generously. But to infer that God requires people to live at a subsistence level and deny themselves any comforts or luxuries is an unfounded stretch. Furthermore, living frugally as a way to conceal one's fear or guilt over money certainly doesn't glorify God. When you consider everything the Bible has to say about money, it's difficult to conclude categorically that all people who love God are supposed to be poor.

As a child, I had difficulty embracing what I learned about money in Sunday school. I didn't like the idea of being poor. Having been raised in a stable, middle-class family, I didn't know anything about poverty. I wasn't poor and I didn't want to be poor. I couldn't imagine living with less than I had. Quite to the contrary, I was ambitious when it came to success and money, and I craved to have even more—more things, better things, nicer things.

So I transitioned into young adulthood with my sights set very high. I was in essence saying, "Jesus, you may not have been rich, but one day I definitely will be!" As I will share with you later, my obsession with acquiring wealth, power, and prestige would lead to a personal crisis over the issue of what I loved most: God or money.

I Pray That You May Prosper
On the other side of the great divide on the topic of money and wealth are

a growing number of Christians who believe that God wants believers to seek and enjoy material abundance. This segment of the church concludes from their view of Scripture that God's followers, especially those who give generously and sacrificially to his ministries, can have anything and everything they want. Some go so far as to claim that God wills the material prosperity of every Christian, so living with little instead of much is going outside his will. And since God has willed that Christians live in abundance and luxury, these believers seek to bring glory to God by always going first class. They want the top of the line and the biggest and best of everything.

This view of money, wealth, and material possessions finds its loudest voices among those who propagate "the prosperity gospel" or "prosperity teaching." An important text in their argument is 3 John 2, where the apostle John greeted his reader Gaius with the words "Beloved, I pray that you may prosper in all things and be in health, just as your soul prospers" (NKJV). They see in this verse a blank check signed by God for any and every kind of prosperity, including unlimited financial and material wealth.

Other "biblical proofs" cited by the God-wants-us-rich proponents include the following:

1. The abundant life.

Jesus said, "I have come that they may have life, and have it to the full" (John 10:10). Living life to the full—the abundant life—is interpreted by the God-wants-us-rich segment to include monetary and material abundance as well as spiritual abundance. If Jesus wants us rich in every way, there is no limit to the wealth we can amass and enjoy.

The abundant material life translates differently for different people, from the mentality of enjoying nice things whenever possible to the aggressive approach of working every financial angle in order to continuously ratchet up one's quality of life. But for most people on this side of the divide, there is nothing wrong with earning a lot of money and using some of it for frills and luxuries. When it comes to a sport-utility vehicle, a Chevy Tahoe is nice but a Lincoln Navigator is *really* nice. Why not go for really nice when you can afford it? Off-the-rack apparel is fine, but a few custom-made suits or couture dresses in the wardrobe are a real treat.

2. Wealthy role models.

A fair number of the major characters in the Bible were both godly and wealthy. The first three patriarchs of Israel—Abraham, Isaac, and Jacob—were the lords of huge estates, possessing land, flocks, herds, and servants. Even Joseph, who was sold into slavery by his brothers, rose to the number-two position of power and wealth in Egypt. And then there's King Solomon, the wisest and wealthiest man in the world during his lifetime. Since God blessed exemplary role models with great wealth, many Christians conclude that it is his will for all of us to enjoy material abundance.

3. A lavish God.

When God spoke the universe into existence, he spared no expense in abundance and variety of features: plants, animals, mountains, plains, stars, planets, moons, etc. When he commanded the building of the tabernacle, and later the temple, he enlisted the best craftsmen and specified the finest materials, including precious metals and stones, elegant fabrics, and rich designs and ornamentation.

Exodus 28 describes the sacred garments God ordained for the priests of Israel, beginning with Aaron and his sons, to give them dignity and honor. These ornate vestments were crafted using finely twisted linen, richly colored embroidery, precious stones in gold filigree settings, and chains, rings, and bells made of pure gold. Since believers are referred to in the Bible as "a royal priesthood" (1 Peter 2:9), beautiful, expensive clothes seem to be appropriate for our station as the recipients of God's abundance.

In contrast to their brothers and sisters who seek to glorify God by limiting their income, the God-wants-us-rich contingent seek to glorify God by enjoying the abundant material life that the modern, Western world offers and that they view as their inheritance. They look for ways to keep up with the Joneses, increase their income, and improve their quality of life in every way.

As with the God-wants-us-poor extreme, Christians who tout the idea that God wants all his people to be financially rich (and who use Western standards as the benchmark for what *rich* is) must stretch the counsel of Scripture to validate their point. So if these opposites on the issue of people and wealth both push at the limits of God's Word, where is the middle ground? In other words, what does the Bible really say about how we should acquire, manage, and enjoy money and material possessions? As I consider Scripture on this topic, it appears to me that there is a good deal of middle ground between these two poles.

Expansive Middle Ground

As we read in the Bible, God called and blessed men and women regardless of their economic strata. He chose a rich man, Abraham, to found the nation of Israel, and he chose a peasant girl, Mary, to give birth to his beloved Son. God lavished on some of his people great abundance; in the case of others, he provided only for their basic needs of food and clothing. Let's consider a biblical example from each end of the spectrum: King Solomon and the apostle Paul.

If Solomon in his prime were alive today, he would likely be ranked among the world's wealthiest individuals. In March 2007, Forbes.com reported that there were 946 billionaires in the world with a collective net worth of $3.5 trillion. Topping the list were Americans Bill Gates ($56 billion) and Warren Buffett ($52 billion), along with Carlos Slim Helú of Mexico ($49 billion), Ingvar Kamprad of Sweden ($33 billion), and Lakshmi Mittal of India ($32 billion).[1] Translate Solomon's vast wealth from the tenth century B.C. into twenty-first-century dollars, and you might find the wise king right up there with today's financial giants.

How did Solomon acquire his wealth? God gave it to him! You might remember the story from 2 Chronicles 1. God appeared to King Solomon and said, "Ask for whatever you want me to give you" (verse 7). Noble Solomon asked for wisdom and knowledge for governing the nation of Israel. God responded, "Since this is your heart's desire and you have not asked for wealth, riches or honor,…therefore wisdom and knowledge will be given you. And I will also give you wealth, riches and honor, such as no king who was before you ever had and none after you will have" (verses 11-12).

Listing 2007's wealthiest royals and rulers, Forbes.com started with Abdullah Bin Abdulaziz, the king of Saudi Arabia, worth an estimated $21 billion. If God literally meant that Solomon's wealth would be greater than that of every other ruler in history, the commensurate net worth of Israel's king would have exceeded King Abdullah's. And God didn't have a problem with it. Rather, he blessed Solomon with wealth and prestige beyond our comprehension, even though Solomon's devotion to God waned in his later years.

And then, offering a stark contrast, there was the apostle Paul. This man was arguably the most influential servant of Christ in the history of the church. If God universally blesses his people with wealth in proportion to their devotion to him, Paul should have been the Bill Gates of his time in terms of net worth. But in reality the great apostle lived nearer the other end of the financial scale. Little is known about Paul's financial status prior to his conversion. Since he was thought to have been well educated in the Jewish tradition, he may have come from a wealthy family. But in the service of Christ he was an itinerant preacher and church planter, living off his part-time earnings as a tentmaker plus the financial and material gifts of friends and parishioners.

In one of his later letters Paul reminded his readers of his impressive résumé as a follower of Judaism before meeting Christ. Yet no matter what material advantages he may have enjoyed from his upbringing and training, the apostle declared, "I consider everything a loss compared to the surpassing greatness of knowing Christ Jesus my Lord, *for whose sake I have lost all things.* I consider them rubbish, that I may gain Christ" (Philippians 3:8; emphasis added). Financial and material gain was not important to Paul. Everything he acquired and possessed was expendable for the cause of Christ.

Apparently Paul experienced the financial roller coaster ride many of us experience. There were fat times and lean times in Paul's financial life. He testified in the same letter, "I know what it is to be in need, and I know what it is to have plenty. I have learned the secret of being content in any and every situation, whether well fed or hungry, whether living in plenty or in want" (Philippians 4:12).

Solomon, the great king, may have lived his entire life without ever being in want for anything financially. But Paul, the great apostle, apparently lived in want at times and may never have been what we would call wealthy. This diversity appears to be common throughout biblical and church history. Paul promised, "My God will meet all your needs according to his glorious riches in Christ Jesus" (Philippians 4:19). Sometimes God satisfies our hunger with a lavish banquet; sometimes it's a crust of bread. Sometimes God provides a castle; sometimes it's a studio apartment. Many times God provides for our needs through the hard work of our jobs; occasionally an unexpected check arrives in the mail for just the right amount.

God's supply may be superabundant, generous, or barely enough. But in this broad middle ground between the God-wants-us-poor and God-wants-us-rich extremes, God takes care of his own in his way and in his time.

Quality above Quantity

God clearly isn't anxious or concerned about his people being rich or poor or any shade in between. He doesn't seem to focus on how much or how little his people acquire and enjoy. But he does seem intently focused on his relationship with his people and how our desire to acquire and distribute assets impacts that relationship. In other words, God is not as interested in our financial and material bottom line as in how we feel about him and whether we are willing to put our relationship with the Lord ahead of our desire to acquire and distribute money. I call this approach to money and possessions "creating eternal wealth." Eternal wealth is an issue of quality of relationship over quantity of money.

As the term suggests, eternal wealth must be viewed with an eternal perspective, not a temporal one. Multimillionaire Malcolm Forbes, publisher of *Forbes*, America's first business magazine, is said to have coined the saying "He who dies with the most toys wins." This quip is the mantra of the temporal perspective of wealth for those who live to acquire and enjoy all they can in this life. And if this life is all we get, then we have every reason to join them in the frantic pursuit to grab all we can and eat, drink, and be merry.

However, the seventy-, eighty-, or ninety-odd years you may live on this planet aren't all you get. In fact, they are only a tiny fraction of the life that God has planned for those who love him. So living and earning and saving and spending for this life only is a tragically shortsighted approach to the use of our resources. Forbes's mantra would be better stated, "He who dies with the most toys alone wins nothing."

Eternal wealth views financial and material wealth from Jesus' perspective: "Do not store up for yourselves treasures on earth, where moth and rust destroy, and where thieves break in and steal. But store up for yourselves treasures in heaven, where moth and rust do not destroy, and where thieves do not break in and steal. For where your treasure is, there your heart will be also" (Matthew 6:19-21). It's not what you accumulate and enjoy here that counts; it's what you accumulate and utilize here for God's purposes that benefits you and his kingdom the most. Or to paraphrase Malcolm Forbes's line again, those who die having loved the Lord and used their resources for him and his kingdom win everything!

Freedom with Responsibility

The Bible allows us the freedom to create wealth without limit. But with that freedom comes the sobering responsibility to discover his purposes for wealth and to use our wealth to fulfill God's purposes on earth. Our freedom to create wealth is easily corrupted when we fail to be accountable to God and to others for the wealth we acquire.

It would, of course, be easier to ignore the responsibility that God's freedom brings. In his book *The Burden of Freedom*, Bible teacher and bestselling author Dr. Myles Munroe states that freedom is more difficult than slavery because it demands more of us than oppression demands.[2] Munroe argues that our freedom in Christ is often misunderstood by people who view it as license to live without laws and accountability. But if we take that path, we are doomed to become slaves to our money and possessions and to suffer the consequences of a strained relationship with God.

In the Garden of Eden, God said to Adam and Eve, "Be fruitful and increase in number; fill the earth and subdue it" (Genesis 1:28). Later God instructed them, "You are free to eat from any tree in the garden; but you must not eat from the tree of the knowledge of good and evil" (Genesis 2:16-17). These passages illustrate that God extends great freedom for creative endeavor within boundaries of accountability for our actions. Accountability mandates that we manage the things we produce in such a way that we dominate them instead of the things dominating us. It also sets limits so that while all things may be accessible to us, we are not to participate in all things.

God gives us the freedom to choose what to do with our money. But we are forever accountable to God so that our prosperity always happens under God's sovereign jurisdiction and within the confines of the Lord's eternal authority. God is pleased to have us prosper and control the material things of this world as long as we do so in accordance with his will. We were never meant to be enslaved by the world's principles, socioeconomic systems, or ways of thinking about material things, including money. God designed us to rule over these things while submitting to his ultimate authority.

It should come as no surprise that the subject of money creates such controversy in our lives and the church. Money has an energy or power associated with it that can bring out the best or the worst in us. Attitudes of covetousness, greed, fear, and guilt, as well as generosity, compassion, and hope, can all be affected by money. Creating eternal wealth is a matter of economics, but this wealth is also a byproduct of our character and our relationship with and accountability to God. As we explore the principles of eternal wealth, we will begin to understand that eternal wealth results as we invest spiritually and economically the resources God has invested in us. Eternal wealth is a reflection of the right choices we make with our freedom to choose what to do with our potential and our money. Creating eternal wealth is a matter of loving God, loving others as ourselves, and making money.

QUESTIONS FOR REFLECTION AND DISCUSSION

1. How would you characterize your church's teaching on the subject of wealth and money?

2. In what ways has your understanding of God's will for your prosperity been shaped by the things you learned in church?

3. Do you believe God wants you to have and manage large amounts of economic resources? Why or why not?

> Creating eternal wealth is a consequence, not a goal.

Chapter 2

PRINCIPLES OF ETERNAL WEALTH

My journey to embracing God's principles for eternal wealth was long and painful. That wasn't God's fault; I had my own agenda when it came to money. In order to set the stage for a full explanation of eternal wealth, allow me to share another segment of my story that illustrates why I was such a tough nut for God to crack.

My perception from Sunday school that Christians were supposed to be poor didn't mesh with my hopes of becoming wealthy. Even as a young girl, I was captivated by the culture's system for acquiring an abundance of money and possessions. I believed that the American Dream was mine for the taking. So I quietly decided that I was not going to be poor like Jesus. I was going to be rich.

It didn't take long for me to discover that achieving the American Dream would be more of a struggle than I had anticipated. I entered the University of California–Davis with my sights set on the most affluent and prestigious career I could think of: medicine. My intention to become a medical doctor had little to do with helping people and a great deal to do with the income I could generate and the prestige that comes with having M.D. after one's name. But I was not prepared to focus on the academic challenges of the pre-med major. Instead, I got heavily involved in the party scene, and the best I could muster academically was a C+ average. When it came time to apply for medical school, my transcript was an embarrassment, and my misplaced motives could not be hidden. So I withdrew my application and got the best job I could find, even though the income from that job was a far cry from the earnings of a doctor.

Several years later I began a personal relationship with Jesus Christ by inviting him into my life. As I began my walk with Christ, I also discovered my attraction to accounting and redirected my attempt to create wealth into the fields of business, accounting, and economics. I entered the business program at California State University–Hayward to become a certified public accountant, poured my heart and soul into pursuing my new career, and loved every minute of it. I studied diligently and excelled academically, maintaining an A average. At age thirty-one I passed the CPA exam on my first attempt.

After passing the CPA exam, it was simply a matter of deciding which of the "big eight" public accounting firms I wanted to work for. I applied to six of them and received job offers from all six. I selected Price Waterhouse. The other accountants joining the firm from undergraduate school were much younger than I was, but I didn't care. I was proud of my delayed success and had no problem with long, intense hours of work.

Having failed to become a doctor, I was determined to become an influential and wealthy businesswoman. I no longer had to conceal my desire to make money, because everybody I worked with had the same goal. I had high hopes for a prosperous future and wasn't going to let anything get in my way. So when I became pregnant four months after starting at Price Waterhouse, I decided to work as long as I was able, give birth, and then return to the office as soon as possible.

It broke my heart to leave my son, Jonathan, with my aunt every day after a brief maternity leave. But the desire to advance my prestigious career overpowered the desire to care for Jonathan myself. I toughened my resolve for career success and financial prosperity, buried my secret yearning to be a stay-at-home mom, and headed back to work. My husband, Terence, and I were growing Christians, and we had even started giving regularly to the church, both with finances and through volunteer work. But our priority was clearly the fast track to success and affluence we were on. I had no idea that God would have to derail my runaway train to riches in order to turn my heart fully to him and my family.

In the meantime I continued my climb to the top. After a few years at Price Waterhouse, followed by several years of working for a large telecommunications company, I accepted a financial position with a cable television company in San Francisco. I'd finally received my first six-figure salary, and the next year I was awarded a 50 percent increase. Opportunities for advancement and greater income in my career appeared on the horizon. I was well on my way to achieving the financial goals that dominated my life at that point.

By 1999, twelve years after starting my CPA career at Price Waterhouse, I had achieved the position of division chief financial officer and vice president of finance at AT&T Broadband in Seattle, Washington. My compensation package of salary and bonuses reached well into six figures, far beyond my starting salary at Price Waterhouse of twenty-seven thousand dollars. The rapid climb to the top much exceeded my dreams.

Relishing every moment of my success, I still wasn't finished. I possessed enormous drive, and I wanted to make even more money. God had been challenging me about elevating prestige, career success, and wealth above him and my family, but I refused to listen. God didn't have an issue with my success and large salary; they weren't the problem. The problem was that, during the later years of my career success, pride slipped in and I began pursuing goals on my terms instead of his. I had allowed myself to be controlled by things God had created and commanded me to control under his authority. Had it not been for God's gracious but painful intervention in my life, my continued ascent in the business and financial world would have earned me wealth but taken me far from God.

> **Eternal Wealth Defined**
>
> Eternal wealth is the wealth we accrue when our pursuit of an intimate relationship with God compels us to maximize our potential, fulfill our purpose, and invest economic and human resources for the benefit of God's economy.

In the pages ahead I will tell you what happened to me next. But first I need to solidify the biblical foundation for creating eternal wealth. The intervention of God's humbling love and liberating truth set me on the path to creating wealth in a supernatural dimension. It can do the same for you.

The Bible's Foundation for Creating Eternal Wealth

The measure of success for creating eternal wealth is not how much money we are able to acquire. Success is measured by how we choose to *respond* to the economic resources we acquire and how we choose to use our gifts and abilities in the world. Creating eternal wealth is a matter of good stewardship, the kind of stewardship that results from the following:

- An intimate relationship with God
- A deep level of trust in God's Word
- Depth of character and an understanding of purpose
- Effective management of business and economic resources
- Wisdom for leadership and building relationships
- A commitment to using our resources to advance God's economy in the world

The correlation between our relationship with God and good stewardship over money and economic power is concisely captured in my definition of eternal wealth: *Eternal wealth is the wealth we accrue when our pursuit of an intimate relationship with God compels us to maximize our potential, fulfill our purpose, and invest economic and human resources for the benefit of God's economy.*

Before I define what I mean by good stewardship, let me comment briefly on this description of eternal wealth.

First, eternal wealth is something every person may produce. Producing eternal wealth is not, however, an end in itself but rather is the by-product of the pursuit of a higher goal: obtaining the gift of an eternal, intimate relationship with God in Christ Jesus.

Second, eternal wealth—as the name indicates—is eternal. We realize and enjoy some benefits from our investing in this life, but the richest dividends are the true riches we will realize and enjoy throughout eternity.

Third, God wants us to develop our potential and fulfill our life's purpose no matter what type of work we do. When we fail to fulfill our purpose, we waste the potential God gives us.

Fourth, it is okay to multiply and increase resources. I believe that God not only permits us but encourages us to be as industrious and resourceful as we can in generating material and financial assets. God wants us to succeed in the work we do, and successful work produces increasing economic benefits.

Fifth, it is our generous, and at times sacrificial, investment of our resources into the lives of others that provides the capital for God's economy. God's economy is simply his economic plan for the distribution of goods and resources that will fulfill the desires of his heart by building the lives of people who live in his kingdom.

Creating eternal wealth happens when we learn how to effectively steward the resources we possess. A steward is a person who manages another person's household, property, finances, or affairs. In the parable of the three servants, found in the Gospel of Matthew, Jesus used a story about money and investing to illustrate that his followers must be diligent to use their gifts and abilities in a manner that meets his expectations. This story has a much broader application to our lives than money and wealth, but it certainly doesn't exclude these elements. And with regard to money and wealth, it establishes key principles of stewardship for creating eternal wealth.

> The Kingdom of Heaven can be illustrated by the story of a man going on a trip. He called together his servants and gave them money to invest for him while he was gone. He gave five bags of gold to one, two bags of gold to another, and one bag of gold to the last—dividing it in proportion to their abilities—and then left on his trip. The servant who received the five bags of gold began immediately to invest the money and soon doubled it. The servant with two bags of gold also went right to work and doubled the money. But the servant who received the one bag of gold dug a hole in the ground and hid the master's money for safekeeping.
>
> After a long time their master returned from his trip and called them to give an account of how they had used his money. The servant to whom he had entrusted the five bags of gold said, "Sir, you gave me five bags of gold to invest, and I have doubled the amount." The master was full of praise. "Well done, my good and faithful servant. You have been faithful in handling this small amount, so now I will give you many more responsibilities. Let's celebrate together!"
>
> Next came the servant who had received the two bags of gold, with the report, "Sir, you gave me two bags of gold to invest, and I have doubled the amount." The master said, "Well done, my good

and faithful servant. You have been faithful in handling this small amount, so now I will give you many more responsibilities. Let's celebrate together!"

Then the servant with the one bag of gold came and said, "Sir, I know you are a hard man, harvesting crops you didn't plant and gathering crops you didn't cultivate. I was afraid I would lose your money, so I hid it in the earth and here it is."

But the master replied, "You wicked and lazy servant! You think I'm a hard man, do you, harvesting crops I didn't plant and gathering crops I didn't cultivate? Well, you should at least have put my money into the bank so I could have some interest. Take the money from this servant and give it to the one with the ten bags of gold. To those who use well what they are given, even more will be given, and they will have an abundance. But from those who are unfaithful, even what little they have will be taken away. Now throw this useless servant into outer darkness, where there will be weeping and gnashing of teeth." (Matthew 25:14-30, NLT)

This story illustrates two contrasting types of stewardship: good and faithful stewardship versus wicked and lazy stewardship. It reflects an expectation from God that we use every ability and resource at our disposal in a productive way. God measures productivity by the degree to which we work to increase the resources we've stewarded and the degree to which we return those resources to him. Our willingness or unwillingness to acknowledge God as our Master and to invest and distribute our money, material resources, and work effort to benefit his kingdom is a reflection of our stewardship, and our stewardship reflects the type of relationship we have with God. If we choose rightly, our diligence in serving God with our work, our money, and our possessions will not only benefit us materially in this life but will also store up for us great treasure in heaven—eternal wealth. If we choose wrongly, we store up nothing of eternal value, and suffer the unpleasant results.

I draw from this story and other Bible passages seven foundational principles of stewardship for creating eternal wealth.

Principle 1: Resources for creating eternal wealth come from God.

The master in the story is about to leave on a journey. He wants his financial portfolio to keep growing in his absence, so he summons three trusted servants, gives each of them a large sum of cash, and commissions them to invest the money and turn a profit.

Each bag of gold in the story was a talent, which was equivalent to 1,200 ounces. As I write this chapter, the price of gold is approximately $621 per ounce. So in today's economy each bag of gold would be worth at least $745,000! Even the servant who received one bag of gold was richly endowed.

To whom did the money belong? Clearly it belonged to the master. To whom did the servants belong? They were the master's too, not slaves kept against their will but stewards with differing abilities and the freedom to choose whether and how they would contribute to the master's business. If any of the servants was tempted to claim credit for any good that came out of the financial endeavor, he need only remember that he couldn't accomplish anything without having first received the master's money and trust.

Our Master, Jesus, is presently on a "trip." He ascended to heaven after his death and resurrection, leaving us to conduct his business—loving people, making disciples, and building his kingdom—until his return. The entire operation is his, including the resources we possess and invest. You may think the paycheck you bring home every week is yours because it was your blood, sweat, and tears that earned it. But where did your blood, sweat, and tears come from? God gave them to you. Where did your ability to effectively engage in business come from? God gave it to you. Where did your ambition, zeal, and inspiration to work hard and achieve your goals come from? God gave them to you. God is the source of your life, intelligence, physical strength, special talents, unique abilities, personality, and so on. Whether you acknowledge God or not, you couldn't earn a dime without him.

King David wrote, "The earth is the LORD's, and everything in it, the world, and all who live in it" (Psalm 24:1). Paul declared, "If we live, we live to the Lord; and if we die, we die to the Lord. So, whether we live or die, we belong to the Lord" (Romans 14:8). Since we are Christ's servants, everything we have and handle belongs to our Master. Creating eternal wealth begins when we humbly acknowledge that all resources we receive from and manage for God belong entirely to him.

Principle 2: We are accountable to God for how we use his resources.

The master in Jesus' parable gave his servants bags of money to invest for him. When he returned from his trip, the master called for an accounting of what his stewards had gained for him with his money. The investment capital belonged to the master, so he had an undeniable interest in how it was managed and the level of return he received.

Eternal wealth accrues as we understand that the profits generated from our talents and resources are not only ours but also God's—and then operate accordingly by managing the profits in a manner that fulfills the desires of God's heart. Christ's followers are to use their gifts, skills, and abilities, including those we employ to generate material wealth, to profit God's economy and build his kingdom. The profits we create are intended to benefit us personally *and* fuel God's economy—his plan for managing resources and distributing goods and services to achieve his eternal purposes.

It's not the amount of money and possessions we can amass that's important; it's the attitude we have about our potential, along with the condition of our relationship with and level of accountability to the Master, that counts. Of course, the more successful we are at developing our potential and generating resources, the more generous we can be at funding Christ's work in the world. Yet it is our relationship with our Master, our willingness to submit to his authority and to do the work, that is of ultimate importance to God. He is looking for good and faithful servants who know the Master and diligently and effectively work with whatever amount of resources they've been given.

Principle 3: When we take good care of God's business, God takes good care of us.

The parable Jesus told makes no mention of any salary and bonus package for the three servants. But we do know they were hired to manage the master's financial affairs and were entrusted with the master's finances in proportion to their ability. They obviously were equipped (albeit to differing degrees) and were deeply trusted by the master. It's also probable that they were well compensated by their "employer" commensurate with their respective abilities.

An axiom from the Law of Moses states, "Do not keep an ox from eating as it treads out the grain" (Deuteronomy 25:4, NLT). In other words, the person performing the work should be able to make a living from the work he does. Jesus suggested the same idea when he said, "The worker is worth his keep" (Matthew 10:10). So it is plausible that the three servants benefited financially from managing the master's assets.

Furthermore, the parable hints that the three servants had opportunity to participate in a profit-sharing plan with their employer. The master in the parable stated, "To those who use well what they are given, even more will be given, and they will have an abundance."

The Bible gives us another valuable insight into the master's response. Commending the first two servants, he said, "You have been faithful in handling this small amount, so now I will give you many more responsibilities." He was so thrilled with his servants' work that he promised them more work. As they earned greater levels of responsibility through their diligent efforts, the amount of money they were given to manage increased, and the opportunity for them to share in the profits they generated also increased.

As we create eternal wealth for our Master by acquiring and leveraging resources for his economy, God has graciously promised to meet our needs. Jesus said as much in the Sermon on the Mount: "Do not worry about your life, what you will eat or drink; or about your body, what you will wear" (Matthew 6:25). He went on to say that God, who feeds the birds and clothes the flowers more elegantly than Solomon in all his splendor, will tend to our needs. And Paul was talking about material needs when he promised, "My God will meet all your needs according to his glorious riches in Christ Jesus" (Philippians 4:19).

Furthermore, I think God is just as responsive to reward our diligent efforts in developing our potential and building his economy as we assume the master in the parable was. I see God's generosity in Luke 6:38: "If you give, you will receive. Your gift will return to you in full measure, pressed down, shaken together to make room for more, and running over. Whatever measure you use in giving—large or small—it will be used to measure what is given back to you" (NLT). The gift we give is the work we do that produces results benefiting ourselves and others. When we give this gift, it makes room for goodness to come back to us.

This biblical principle can be illustrated this way: when you serve as a garden hose in God's garden, you can't help but get wet while watering the flowers. In other words, developing our potential enables us to engage in work that produces world-changing results, and world-changing results attract financial capital. It sounds like a divine profit-sharing plan to me!

Practically speaking, this means that as a result of the hard work we do to develop ourselves and to take care of God's business, we will enjoy the resources we are privileged to generate and manage. For example, because of your hard work, you may be able to move to a better neighborhood, buy a larger home for your family, send your kids to private school, or take that special trip you have always wanted to take. What you do with God's blessings is up to you. Just understand that as you work and take care of God's business, God will take care of you.

Principle 4: We have different abilities, so we will have different results from our work.

The parable states that the master divided his money among the servants "according to their abilities." Apparently they were at different levels of talent, expertise, training, and experience. They even may have lived in different towns or countries, with differing economic, social, or cultural conditions. They may have been raised in different types of families or come from different environments. Whatever the origin of their differences, the parable clearly states that the servants did not have equal abilities.

God has given you, or you and your spouse together, certain abilities for earning money and managing what you earn for maximum return. The Lord has empowered you to do great things according to your abilities. When you work hard and make the most of your opportunities by educating yourself and honing your skills and abilities, you will produce resources to enjoy and to invest in your Master's work. However, the amount of resources you produce will not be equal to the amount of resources everyone else produces. We will never all become millionaires, because we do not all possess that level of wealth-producing ability. Nevertheless, we do all possess the ability to produce a significant return on God's investment in us.

I'm not ignoring the fact that some people live and work in hostile environments that can make it harder to produce an increase in what

God has given them. But if you fail to put forth the effort, or if you hold a negative attitude toward life and God's equipping power, simply because you can't produce the level of financial assets that your neighbor can, you won't please God. The two hardworking servants did not give the master equal amounts of money back. The first servant gave the master ten talents back, and the second servant gave the master five talents back. However, they both produced a 100 percent return on the master's initial investment. They maximized their return with regard to their potential, and for that reason they received the master's reward.

The two servants who produced a 100 percent return on the master's initial investment wanted to make a difference for the master. I believe the third servant had a bad attitude and spent too much time worrying about the apparent inequality of their abilities, and in doing so missed his opportunity to make a difference for the master. I believe his bad attitude stemmed from the fatal mistake he made of comparing himself to other people.

Paul wrote, "Whatever you do, work at it with all your heart, as working for the Lord, not for men" (Colossians 3:23). No matter where you come from, where you live now, or what you do for gainful employment, your ultimate employer is the Lord, so you must work to please him. In part that means that, instead of comparing yourself to other people, you should compare yourself to yourself. Are you getting better? Are you producing more this year than last year? Are you growing spiritually, economically, mentally, and socially? Are you using your abilities to fulfill your purpose and doing work that matters to God? Are you seizing each day as an opportunity to change what needs changing in your life so that you can produce results according to your abilities?

Creating eternal wealth happens as we take small steps toward achieving results that leave an undeniable mark on our lives and the lives of those we care about. Creating eternal wealth happens when we use our abilities to produce results reflecting the best work we can do.

Principle 5: We must maximize our potential for God's kingdom.

The servants in the parable had differing abilities, yet each had the same assignment: invest for the master. Likewise, we all have different natural abilities and opportunities for creating wealth. We each come into the Master's service with our own unique assortment of God-given talents, IQ, education, life experience, personality, spiritual gifts, street smarts, and so on. We also come from different backgrounds that can either contribute to or take away from opportunities for creating wealth. Our abilities are a representation of our potential. And God is saying to us, "Use your potential to invest for the Master."

Potential means the ability to become something that doesn't yet exist. Someone has potential when that person has the capacity for growth or development. The master empowered each servant with the potential to grow and produce a return on his investment. Each had freedom to choose how to use his potential and resources. Notice, however, that the two hardworking servants immediately went to work, whereas the third servant did not.

Potential is a reflection of our capacity for production. However, it is our attitude and work ethic that dictate what happens with our potential. We must have a positive attitude about our potential and work hard if we want to make something of our potential. When we are willing to work hard and maintain a positive attitude about work, our circumstances, and our abilities, we are empowered for great success. One of the greatest football coaches in history, Vince Lombardi, said it this way: "The difference between a successful person and others is not a lack of strength, not a lack of knowledge, but rather a lack of will." In other words, no matter what our circumstances, it is our will that determines our future.

The Nobel Prize–winning playwright George Bernard Shaw is quoted as saying, "People are always blaming their circumstances for what they are.

I don't believe in circumstances. The people who get on in this world are the people who get up and look for the circumstances they want, and, if they can't find them, make them." The first two servants in the parable did just that: they got up and looked for the circumstances they wanted and needed in order to produce a return on the master's investment. They worked hard. However, the third servant chose a different response. His negative attitude kept him from producing a return on the master's investment.

The word Jesus used for "abilities" is the Greek word *dunamis*, which is also used in the New Testament for force, miraculous power, strength, and mighty work. You find the same word in Acts 1:8 in connection with the Holy Spirit: "You will receive power [*dunamis*] when the Holy Spirit comes on you; and you will be my witnesses in Jerusalem, and in all Judea and Samaria, and to the ends of the earth." It is also used in Hebrews 11:11, describing how Abraham and Sarah, who were well past childbearing age, were "enabled" (*dunamis*) to produce a son through faith in God's promise. The word occurs again in 2 Corinthians 12:9, when the Lord said to Paul, "My grace is sufficient for you, for my power [*dunamis*] is made perfect in weakness." The positive attitude the first two servants had toward the master, their potential, and his assignment for them ignited their God-given ability (*dunamis*), enabling God's power to work with them to produce an abundant return on his investment. The third servant's negative attitude toward the master, his potential, and his assignment resulted in his quenching his God-given ability (*dunamis*) and wasting the potential he was given.

Creating eternal wealth is at least as much about our attitude toward God and response to his goodness as it is about our natural skills, talents, and opportunities. No matter what you bring to the Lord by way of talents and skills, you will greatly please him if you respond positively to his assignment, thereby enabling the Lord's *dunamis* power to work in you to gain eternal wealth.

Principle 6: God gives eternal rewards for good and faithful service to him.

It's hard to miss the master's great pleasure over the success of his two good and faithful servants. He was generous with his verbal praise: "Well done!" He was generous with his promotions, assuring them of greater responsibilities with greater reward. And he was generous with his joy over their hard work and success. No matter how much wealth God allows you to acquire and enjoy here on earth, the Bible promises even greater rewards of eternal wealth in heaven for your faithful service to God on earth. The Bible talks about our being awarded crowns in heaven: a crown of righteousness (2 Timothy 4:8), a crown of life (James 1:12), and a crown of glory that will never fade away (1 Peter 5:4). You may never become a company president or CEO in this life, but you are guaranteed to live like a king or queen in God's eternal kingdom.

The Bible also talks about the treasures of eternal wealth. Jesus urged us, "Store up for yourselves treasures in heaven, where moth and rust do not destroy, and where thieves do not break in and steal" (Matthew 6:20). Notice that these are treasures for yourself. We're not told what these treasures are, but they clearly surpass earthly treasures because we will enjoy them forever.

The Bible also talks about eternal rewards for our faithful service. Jesus said, "The Son of Man is going to come in his Father's glory with his angels, and then he will reward each person according to what he has done" (Matthew 16:27). Paul wrote, "Serve wholeheartedly, as if you were serving the Lord, not men, because you know that the Lord will reward everyone for whatever good he does" (Ephesians 6:7-8). "Whatever you do, work at it with all your heart, as working for the Lord, not for men, since you know that you will receive an inheritance from the Lord as a reward. It is the Lord Christ you are serving" (Colossians 3:23-24). And in the closing verses of Revelation, the King of kings proclaims, "Behold, I am coming soon! My reward is with me, and I will give to everyone according to what he has done" (Revelation 22:12).

Serving God means engaging in work that matters to God. You may be at a point in your life where you feel that you are underpaid and underappreciated in the work you do. As long as you're working to develop your potential so you can multiply the return on God's investment in your life, you are engaged in work that matters to God. So don't be impatient with small beginnings. Perhaps your boss is a Scrooge when it comes to perks, raises, bonuses, rewards, and other forms of recognition. Maybe you feel like you're doing a thankless job. But remember who you're really working for. The good news is that your ultimate Boss, your Lord and Savior Jesus Christ, is lavish in his appreciation and rewards to his faithful servants. Not one ounce of energy you expend on developing your potential, or one dollar you spend in his name, will escape his notice or fail to prompt his generosity. Furthermore, if you continue to work hard each day in spite of the lack of recognition and rewards you receive, eventually people will begin to acknowledge and take note of the fine work you've done. God will see to it!

Principle 7: Participating wholeheartedly in God's strategy is not an option.

Nobody would want to be in the third servant's shoes. Not only did he miss out on the master's appreciation and generosity, but also he had to face the master's wrath. "You wicked and lazy servant!" blazed the master. All the money the servant had been given was taken from him, and he was tossed out without a penny. This steward began with the same advantages and potential of his fellow workers, proportionate to his abilities. He could have increased his wealth dramatically and enjoyed the master's rewards. What went wrong?

First, he didn't acknowledge and respond to his God-given purpose, which was to use his resources to produce a return on his master's investment.

As a steward, he was duty bound to do what the boss told him to do. But he did the opposite. He shirked his responsibility to the master by burying the money instead of investing it as the master commanded. I think this pictures how some people fail to develop their potential. And I also think it pictures how some people selfishly squander their God-given resources in the world's financial and consumer-oriented system or indulge in lifestyles that satisfy their self-interest while they ignore every opportunity to participate in God's economy by giving to others.

Many of us are so caught up in having things easy, or just having things, that God's priorities for our life and wealth get pushed to the back burner. It takes faith in God and an understanding of his purpose for our life and money to direct our energy and resources into fulfilling his purpose. If you try to operate outside God's purpose, the kingdom of God suffers and so do you.

Second, this servant misunderstood the master's mission and values. He lacked an understanding of his God-given purpose which meant he also lacked vision and so he acted out of fear. He called his master "a hard man, harvesting crops you didn't plant and gathering crops you didn't cultivate." In short, the steward was calling him a thief, accusing him of stealing other people's assets. He may have believed that, by investing the master's resources, he would end up losing more than he gained. Better to simply bury what belonged to the master so that he could return it when his master came back. That way the master wouldn't be able to take from him more than he had received. He stashed the cash instead of putting it to work.

I believe the third servant pictures the problems of fear, self-centered attitudes, and spiritual immaturity that are indications of one's lack of intimacy with God. When you spend all your time thinking about yourself, your financial needs, your business, your desires, and how you can satisfy your wants, you won't have the desire to devote yourself to fulfilling God's plan for your life and money, nor the energy or focus for God's work. Or if you are afraid of losing what you have, you will be slow to venture out in faith and obedience to invest your resources in the lives of others the way God directs you. But the Bible is clear: "Without faith it is impossible to please God, because anyone who comes to him must believe that he exists and that he rewards those who earnestly seek him" (Hebrews 11:6).

If you are a Christian, you are a servant of Jesus Christ, not out of duty but out of love and gratitude for the salvation he provided for you through his death and resurrection. As his steward, you don't have a choice about whether you are to participate wholeheartedly in Jesus' endeavor in the world. He stands ready to empower your abilities by his Spirit, and he will generously reward you with eternal wealth as you faithfully invest your strength and resources in fulfilling your God-given purpose and building God's kingdom. But don't think you can enjoy the blessings of serving under God's care if you refuse to do what he says.

The cover of the September 2006 issue of *Time* magazine asked the question, "Does God want you to be rich?" I believe God wants each of us to be rich in our understanding of who we are and our accountability to him, and when we are rich in that way, we can't help but produce financial results that defy the odds and exceed the imagination. Like the two servants in the parable, we won't all make the same amount of money. However, when we let the seven principles of stewardship for creating eternal wealth become the foundation upon which all our work efforts are built, we will create wealth...on God's terms. And the reason this is important is because God has a plan for our life and our money.

Questions for Reflection and Discussion

1. How has the way you've used your money, skills, and abilities demonstrated successful stewardship of the resources you possess?

2. In what ways does your management of your career and finances already reflect an understanding of the seven stewardship principles for creating eternal wealth?

3. In what ways does your management of your career and finances need to change to better reflect the principles of stewardship for creating eternal wealth?

" Taking care of his family

is God's top priority. "

Chapter 3

GOD'S FAMILY ENTERPRISE

As the twenty-first century began, my dreams of being a wealthy, influential businesswoman were rapidly coming true. In 1999 I landed a high-level position with AT&T Broadband and was pulling down a big salary. The future looked bright in terms of achieving even greater wealth and prestige. I certainly didn't want the ride to end.

Then in February 2000 God intervened in my big plans. A popular Bible teacher was visiting a church in Kirkland, Washington, and I decided to attend. On that Sunday evening, during a powerful time of prayer in the service, God spoke to me audibly. When I say "audibly," I mean I literally heard his voice speaking to me—something that's happened only a few times in my life. In John 10:4 Jesus said that his sheep will follow him "because they know his voice"; as one of his sheep, I recognized Jesus' voice, and it got my full attention.

The Lord said to me, "Julaine, I want you to pour your love into your husband and your home." I knew what God was talking about. From the moment I took my first CPA job at Price Waterhouse, I had been pouring my energies into my career in a near-fanatical pursuit of my high goals. I loved Terence and Jonathan dearly, and by my estimation we had a healthy family and a good life together, but my career was clearly my highest priority. That Sunday evening in church, God pointedly and dramatically directed me to change my priorities.

But at first I didn't change. I was working hard to achieve and sustain the success I craved, and I was making more money than I'd ever dreamed I would make. I didn't even want to consider that God might be telling me to cut back at the office, quit my job, find a less demanding job, or something similar. Furthermore, the way I looked at it, my marriage didn't need a love infusion from me. My husband was happy and so was my son, who was eleven at the time.

Had I put my rationalization into words, it would have sounded like this: "Lord, I know it's your will for me to be successful at the career you've given me. I'm working hard to create the wealth you have empowered me to create, and it has paid off. I have earned prestige along with promotion after promotion, and I'm making big money. We've been able to buy a beautiful home, send Jonathan to the best schools, and save for retirement. In case you haven't noticed, we also pay our tithes and give generous offerings to the church.

"I don't know why you're asking me to focus on my family at this time. Terence can take care of himself; he doesn't need anything more from me. Besides, he wants me to focus on my job and succeed in the marketplace as much as I do. And Jonathan is fine. I have a beautiful family, God, and I don't need to put anything more into that area."

While I may have wanted to fool God into thinking that everything was okay at home, I was terribly wrong. My relationship with my husband was not fine, contrary to what I naively supposed. Terence later confided in me that he had been blindsided by my lofty career goals and insatiable drive to be the best at what I did. He had known that I would eventually make more money than he did as an aeronautical engineer. But when it finally happened, he was unprepared for the harm it caused our relationship.

As I raced past my husband while striving to make my mark, Terence abdicated much of the control in our household to me—a reality I secretly resented. As I later shared with him, I felt that Terence had left me holding the bag on our finances and discipline issues with Jonathan, and this tension put a strain on our marriage. So I used my career success as a shield to my inner discontent with having to "bring home the bacon and fry it up in a pan."

God's command to pour my love into my husband and home was a clarion call for me to stop ignoring the needs of my family. However, I didn't want to deal with it. I ignored God's straightforward message to me. I continued to work a minimum of sixty hours a week. I didn't have time to do what God wanted because I was too busy achieving what I thought I wanted.

Over the next ten months I would experience the pain and emptiness that come from telling God no. That's when I began to learn that creating eternal wealth means more than working hard to make lots of money. It means investing our lives in what God wants—his enterprise and purpose in the world—more than in what we want.

What Is God's Enterprise?

God's enterprise is his business and takes place in his kingdom. God's enterprise concerns people, and the primary structure through which people function is the family. The Merriam-Webster definition of *family* is "the basic unit in society traditionally consisting of two parents rearing their children; *also:* any of various social units differing from but regarded as equivalent to the traditional family, [such as] a single-parent family." In broad terms, a family is any group of people—related by blood or not—who truly care for one another. God's church is a family in his kingdom.

When Jesus was asked to identify the greatest commandment of all, he not only provided the first one but also gave us the second: " 'Love the Lord your God with all your heart and with all your soul and with all your mind.' This is the first and greatest commandment. And the second is like it: 'Love your neighbor as yourself.' All the Law and the Prophets hang on these two commandments" (Matthew 22:37-40). Next to our love for God, which is primary, we are to love and care for people even as we love and care for ourselves.

God commands us to love one another because taking care of his family is God's first priority, and love is what compels us to take care of one another. Loving our spouse, children, relatives, and others is more important to God than the amount of money we make. When money becomes so important to us that we are willing to sacrifice the relationships we have with our family and loved ones in order to get it or keep it, we cross the line dividing the pathway to creating eternal wealth from the pathway to creating worldly wealth. Loving people as we love ourselves is at the heart of God's purposes in the world, so it must be at the heart of our purposes for how we create and use resources.

Love and Respect

With regard to marriage (which was one area of God's concern for me), God has carefully laid the foundation for love and respect. In Ephesians 5:22-24 he established a divine order for marriage when he said the husband is the head of the wife as Christ is the head of the church. There are many implications to this passage of Scripture. Some women take issue with the idea of submitting to their husbands as the "head" of the wife. I know I had problems with this one.

In Ephesians 5:23 the term *head* carries the meaning of "beachhead," as in one who stakes out territory to make everything safe. It has less to do with hierarchy and more to do with mutual partnership among men and women. However, I interpreted *head* as meaning "to have authority over" in the natural sense. And since I made more money than Terence *and* determined how our money was going to be spent, I just couldn't see him as my "head." Money possesses a seductive energy of its own, and that energy generates power. She who makes the most money controls the power, and she who controls the power is the head in the relationship—or so I thought. But that's not what God's Word says.

I recall the time when I first realized I wasn't following God's Word in this regard. Shortly after I stopped working, I decided to start attending the ladies' Bible study at my church. This study was held on Tuesday mornings, so the only women who were able to attend on a regular basis were women who didn't work. On this particular Tuesday morning, we were asked to select from a series of topics and then we broke up into small groups to have Bible study on that topic. I decided to go to the small group on marriage.

When we got into our small group, I began to size up the women. They were what I would describe as "trophy wives." That is, they were wives whose husbands made so much money that, even in today's society where most households need two incomes to survive, these women didn't have to work. To their husbands' credit, by all outward appearances they seemed well taken care of. Their nails were well manicured, their hair was done, and their clothes were in good shape. Those who brought their children enjoyed the benefit of having them watched by volunteers in the church nursery. This Tuesday morning ritual of ladies' Bible study gave these stay-at-home moms a chance to get away from the hectic responsibilities of motherhood for a period of Bible study, prayer, and fellowship with other women.

I felt different from everyone else in the room. My temporary unemployment situation was just that: temporary. In my heart I was still a career woman. I was on "sabbatical," collecting my thoughts, refueling my passion, and—oh yes—focusing on being a wife and mother. My long-term plans were to get back to work (as soon as I could figure out the work I wanted to do).

My feelings of somehow not belonging in this group got worse as the Bible study went on. The leaders, both of whom were married women (one young and one older), opened the session with prayer. They then began sharing their stories about how they had come to love and respect their husbands. They spoke about their husbands with such adoration and praise that I was amazed. Even when the older woman, who had been married for at least forty years, began to share about a time in her marriage when her passion for her husband had waned, it was clear that God had answered her prayers and given her a new heart for her husband.

She described how the passion dial of her heart was turned to Off until the time God intervened and taught her how to love and respect her husband. It took some time, but eventually God turned the passion dial up as far as it could go. She shared how, during this time of change and transition in her marriage, she prayed daily for her husband by reading Psalm 112 and inserting his name everywhere the words "the righteous" appeared. She also read *The Power of a Praying Wife* by Stormie Omartian. Based on what she learned in that book and the prayers she prayed, she fell in love with her husband all over again.

As I listened to her testimony, I knew I had a problem. The attitude of respect these women had for their husbands was vaguely familiar to me. But instead of my being able to relate to their testimony because it touched the reality of my current existence, it resurrected feelings from a time now past, feelings that were somehow locked away like an old memory. My problem wasn't a lack of love for my husband. I love Terence. He is my best friend as well as my lover. But there was definitely a gap between what these ladies were describing and how I currently viewed Terence.

At the core of my issues were money and the power money gave me. When I began to make more money than Terence, I no longer looked to him with the same amount of respect I did when he made more money than I did. My change in attitude was subtle and gradual. But when God shone his light on the situation by first directing me to pour my love into my husband and my home and then exposing me to the wives at the ladies' Bible study, I knew I had to change. It was the first of several humbling experiences God would take me through as he began to position me to create eternal wealth.

I left that Bible study convicted and afraid. I was convicted because I knew that I didn't respect my husband as I should and that I needed to change. And I was afraid because I didn't know if I wanted to change. (I'm not suggesting that I was the only one in my marriage who had issues. My husband is absolutely wonderful and he treats me very well. He is patient, kind, thoughtful, considerate, great at being a father, and dedicated to our marriage and our family. But he's not Jesus and therefore he's not perfect; Terence has issues too. But his issues were not the point here; the point was whether I had the desire to love and respect him the way he deserved to be loved and respected.)

It's also important for me to clarify that earning more money than Terence caused me to begin to lose respect for my husband. But there are other reasons why wives and husbands sometimes stop respecting each other. For example, maybe your expectations for marriage have gone unmet because you expected your husband to make you happy in ways that he hasn't been able or willing to fulfill. Or perhaps you expected your wife to satisfy your needs in ways she hasn't been able or willing to fulfill. Marriage often results in unfulfilled expectations and unmet expectations from our spouses can cause us to lose respect for them. When we stop respecting each other, for whatever reason, the marriage foundation is compromised.

During the next six weeks, I eagerly attended each ladies' Bible study session. God used those sessions to begin the process of changing me and my attitude toward Terence. It began with my confronting the fact that my career success had caused me to exalt myself above my husband. In simple terms, my prideful and arrogant attitude had crept into our marriage. I made the money; I managed the money; I said how the money would be spent (and Terence rarely disagreed). I liked the control all this gave me. Sadly, I allowed the fact that I had the control to lower my level of respect for my husband.

In addition to asking God to forgive me for my self-centered and arrogant attitude, I had to ask Terence to forgive me. At first Terence tried to play it off as if he hadn't noticed a change in my attitude. It was only later that he admitted he was put off by my prideful attitude.

In addition to seeking forgiveness from God and my husband, I began to ask God to show me how to be the kind of wife that he wanted me to be and that Terence needed me to be. I asked God to change me. This was a different kind of prayer for me because, prior to this point, my prayers for my marriage were always for God to change my husband. I could see the speck in his eye but couldn't see the plank in my own eye.

God used the Tuesday morning ladies' Bible study and the book *The Power of a Praying Wife* (I recommend it to every married woman) to begin the process of making me over into a godly wife. I learned that no matter how much money I'm blessed to make, how much power I wield in the marketplace, or how much prestige my career brings me, God expects me to love *and respect* my husband.

Now, some husbands use Ephesians 5:22-24 as justification for mistreating their wives. Examination of all the issues accompanying application of these verses and exploration of the many ways husbands and wives can show respect for each other would require writing another book. However, the point here remains that even when a woman is gifted to create more wealth in the marketplace than her husband, God expects her to honor and respect her husband. And a woman can't do that if her attitude towards her husband has been tainted by the seduction of money.

The Virtuous Woman

Proverbs 14:1 says, "The wise woman builds her house, but the foolish pulls it down with her hands" (NKJV). How does a woman build her house? With the work she performs to take care of her husband and her home. Taking care of her husband and family, the family finances, and the general affairs of the household is part of the wife's duties.

The virtuous woman described in Proverbs 31:10-31 sets the standard for every working woman to follow. She gets up before sunrise and works all day; she doesn't like to be idle. She cooks for her family, operates a profitable business, owns real estate, takes care of a vineyard, clothes her children, spends money wisely, and furnishes her house well. She has command of her spirit and is able to manage her employees. Balancing her home and work responsibilities isn't easy. However, her strength comes through wisdom, grace, and the fear of God. She is so good at what she does that her husband puts his total trust in her and is confident that she will take good care of his affairs. And she respects her husband.

The virtuous woman of Proverbs 31 is prosperous. But she doesn't allow her prosperity to get in the way of her respect for her husband. Her focus is never selfish; it is always to take care of her husband, her children, and her household.

A wise woman builds her house, but with her own hands the foolish one tears hers down. How does a foolish wife tear down her house? With her own hands. And I will also add, with her mouth.

Most successful women are strong communicators. We are able to exercise the power of persuasive and decisive communication. This leadership trait serves us well in the marketplace and contributes to our career and financial success. But, ladies, when we come into the house, we need to remember that we are no longer the leader of an organization; we're a partner in a household. And if you make more money than your husband, that doesn't make him your subordinate; he's your partner. Therefore, using your powerful communication skills to argue your point in a manner that reflects an attitude of superiority stemming from the fact that you earn more money than your husband will never build your relationship. Watch your words and avoid using an authoritative tone with your husband. And no matter how strongly you may feel about a subject, some things are better left unsaid. Ask God to let you know when it's better to pray, not say. Respecting your husband's position may require you to stop talking and instead exercise the power of a praying wife.

A foolish wife can tear down her house with the work she performs when she foolishly thinks that her prosperity is earned in isolation. Regardless of how independent your career or financial prosperity may get you to think you are, you were not made in isolation. Others have invested in you via the words they have spoken and the deeds they have performed, helping to make you who you are. And hopefully that includes your husband.

Making a good income may give you a feeling of independence, and you may consciously or subconsciously send your husband that message. But money won't comfort you when you need comforting, make you laugh when you need cheering up, love you when you need a warm and gentle touch, or guide you when you're not sure which way to turn. But hopefully your husband will—and does. A foolish wife can tear down her house when she doesn't let her husband know she needs him. Letting our husbands know we need them is one way of showing them respect.

During my rise to the top of the corporate ladder, my career focus was so intense that I slowly began to ignore my husband. God's clarion call to me to pour my love into my husband was also God's wake-up call for me to pay attention to what my husband was going through and how he was processing my success. It was God's call to me not to take my husband for granted and to stop behaving as though I didn't need him.

Ephesians 5:33 says that each husband must love his wife as he loves himself and that the wife must respect her husband. I believe there is a love-respect connection established by this scripture: as women show their husbands respect, husbands demonstrate their love for their wives and vice versa. A foolish wife will ignore this paradigm, and by doing so, she will tear her house down with her hands.

The Danger of Failure amid Success

God's enterprise is the family, and from his point of view, his Word is the charter and the bylaws by which his enterprise is to be governed. Husbands and wives create eternal wealth when they love and respect each other more than any amount of money, power, or prestige they may be blessed to have.

Career success can become a wedge between us and our spouse if we let it. I believe God will intervene in our plans for career success and financial prosperity when we allow the success we experience in the marketplace to interfere with the relationship we have with our spouse and children. God wants marriages and families strengthened and restored so that his enterprise can flourish.

You can work hard to achieve career success and financial prosperity and in the process lose everything that is dear to you if you don't allow God's principles for love and respect to be the foundation upon which you build your relationship with your spouse. Money, power, and prestige are not more valuable in the kingdom of God than strong families. Creating eternal wealth involves making and managing money, but what you do in the workplace will never be more important than the work you do at home.

Taking care of his family enterprise is God's top priority. However, the scope of God's enterprise that we are to concern ourselves with is not limited to our immediate family. As illustrated by the character of the virtuous woman, our concern must extend to taking care of the needs of other people in the world if we want to create eternal wealth. In Proverbs 31:20 we learn that in addition to working inside and outside the home, running a profitable business and earning an income, the virtuous woman "opens her arms to the poor and extends her hands to the needy." In the next chapter we will explore God's mission in his enterprise in the world and see how we can link our pursuit of career and financial success to the fulfillment of that mission through the concern we show for others.

Questions for Reflection and Discussion

1. Pursuing career success at the expense of family relationships is easier to do than many people think. Reflect on your personal career choices and how they have either added to or subtracted from your family's happiness.

2. What changes do you feel God is prompting you to make in order to fulfill his purpose as it pertains to your family?

> Your money has a mission:
>
> seeking and saving that which was lost.

Chapter 4

GOD'S ENTERPRISE IN THE WORLD

God's concern for how we make and manage money and allow our pursuit of financial prosperity to impact our relationships extends beyond marriage and the home. Generally speaking, God is concerned about our relationship with money and our understanding of the purpose for our prosperity. He is concerned about the extent to which we link the purpose for prosperity to the fulfillment of his universal purpose for humankind. God wants us to use money in a manner that fulfills that purpose.

When our relationship with money and understanding of the purpose for prosperity don't enable us to show love beyond the satisfaction of self-centered desires or interest, we set ourselves up to misuse whatever prosperity we achieve. Mohandas Gandhi put it like this: "Capital as such is not evil; it is the wrong use that is evil." Woodrow Wilson said, "You are not here merely to make a living. You are here in order to enable the world to live more amply, with greater vision, with a finer spirit of hope and achievement. You are here to enrich the world, and you impoverish yourself if you forget that errand." These words of motivation spoken by these two world leaders succinctly express the fact that unless we use money and power to help the world become a better place to live and to do good, first in our immediate families and then across the communities and the world we serve, then we misunderstand the purpose for financial prosperity.

The Lord gave us an obvious clue about what he would like us to do with the wealth we're able to produce when he said that we are to love our neighbor as ourselves. Scripture presents two overlapping, inseparable aspects of God's love for people in the world, and our financial prosperity provides one means for us to express that love. I'll call these two aspects of love God's *mission of mercy* and God's *mission of grace*. Generally speaking, the mission of mercy is aimed at meeting people's physical needs, while the mission of grace is aimed at meeting people's spiritual needs. I want to discuss these two aspects separately, but in reality God is concerned about the person as a whole—body, soul, and spirit—and so must we be. In fact, the purpose for our pursuit of career success and financial prosperity should be linked to serving the needs of God's enterprise if we want to create eternal wealth.

The Mission of Mercy

The mission of God's enterprise of mercy is to meet the universal human needs for love, food, shelter, safety, respect, kindness, and justice. Throughout Scripture we see his heart of compassion for people who are neglected, downtrodden, victimized, helpless, and oppressed by people or systems that control economic, political, and social power. God directs us to use all the means at our disposal to care for hurting people in practical ways. Our concern for the needs of others is to be the same as our concern for our families and ourselves when we are hurting, because Jesus commanded us to love our neighbor as we love ourselves.

When Jesus was discussing the two great commandments to love God and love one's neighbor, an expert in the law asked him, "Who is my neighbor?" (Luke 10:29). Jesus answered with the parable of the Good Samaritan (verses 30-37). The story is about a Samaritan who ministers to the physical needs of a Jew who has been beaten, robbed, and left for dead on the roadside. The Good Samaritan sacrifices his time, energy, and money to do the right thing for this unfortunate Jewish traveler.

The Samaritan's actions are noteworthy because, historically, these two races hated each other. Jews viewed Samaritans as lower-class citizens socially, economically, and religiously. They avoided contact with each other. For the Samaritan to look past these ethnic and cultural barriers and help the unfortunate traveler, his commitment to demonstrate kindness and justice had to supersede the hatred between these two races.

What the robbers did to the traveler was wrong. What the religious leaders in the story did by walking past the man instead of helping him was wrong. What the Samaritan did was right, loving, and merciful. And it demonstrates that when it comes to fulfilling God's enterprise of mercy, he expects our compassion to cross all social, economic, political, cultural, and ethnic boundaries.

Perhaps the most vivid picture of our mission of mercy is found in the parable Jesus told to his disciples right after the parable of the three servants. It's called the parable of the sheep and the goats, found in Matthew 25:31-46.

> When the Son of Man comes in his glory, and all the angels with him, he will sit on his throne in heavenly glory. All the nations will be gathered before him, and he will separate the people one from another as a shepherd separates the sheep from the goats. He will put the sheep on his right and the goats on his left.
>
> Then the King will say to those on his right, "Come, you who are blessed by my Father; take your inheritance, the kingdom prepared for you since the creation of the world. For I was hungry and

you gave me something to eat, I was thirsty and you gave me something to drink, I was a stranger and you invited me in, I needed clothes and you clothed me, I was sick and you looked after me, I was in prison and you came to visit me."

Then the righteous will answer him, "Lord, when did we see you hungry and feed you, or thirsty and give you something to drink? When did we see you a stranger and invite you in, or needing clothes and clothe you? When did we see you sick or in prison and go to visit you?"

The King will reply, "I tell you the truth, whatever you did for one of the least of these brothers of mine, you did for me."

Then he will say to those on his left, "Depart from me, you who are cursed, into the eternal fire prepared for the devil and his angels. For I was hungry and you gave me nothing to eat, I was thirsty and you gave me nothing to drink, I was a stranger and you did not invite me in, I needed clothes and you did not clothe me, I was sick and in prison and you did not look after me."

They also will answer, "Lord, when did we see you hungry or thirsty or a stranger or needing clothes or sick or in prison, and did not help you?"

He will reply, "I tell you the truth, whatever you did not do for one of the least of these, you did not do for me."

Then they will go away to eternal punishment, but the righteous to eternal life.

In the parable Jesus pictured his return at the end of time and the final judgment that will then occur. He will separate all of humanity into two groups. One group he identified with terms such as "sheep," "you who are blessed by my father," and "the righteous." When Jesus refers to sheep, he is talking about his devoted followers. Clearly, in the parable, this group represents those who serve Jesus obediently in this life. The other group he referred to as "goats" and "you who are cursed." Jesus never calls his followers goats. These are obviously the unrighteous, those who do not serve God.

How did Jesus distinguish between these two categories of people? By their actions, just as the master in the parable of the three servants distinguished between his servants by the work they performed, or failed to perform, for their master. The parable of the sheep and the goats reveals how God's people are to invest their energies, abilities, money, and other resources in loving service to him. We are to do the right thing by showing mercy to people who are needy and hurting.

When Jesus concluded the parable of the Good Samaritan, this brief exchange took place.

Jesus said, "Which of these three do you think was a neighbor to the man who fell into the hands of robbers?"

The expert in the law replied, "The one who had mercy on him."

Jesus told him, "Go and do likewise" (Luke 10:36-37).

Mercy is compassionate care. We are to be on the alert for people in need of mercy and justice and do what we can to provide help and relief. In the parable of the sheep and the goats, the list Jesus gave represents the kinds of hurting people who spark his compassion and should also spark ours. As Jesus stated in the parable, our highest motivation in the mission of mercy is to serve others as if we were serving him. The late Mother Teresa, one of the great saints of merciful ministry in Christ's name, often prayed, "Dearest Lord, may I see you today and every day in the person of your sick, and, whilst nursing them, minister unto you."[1]

We need to use our money and resources to serve the needs of hungry and hurting people by providing food, shelter, compassionate care, healing, and liberation. But in order to fully meet their needs, we also need to address the root causes of these hurtful situations, including challenging the unjust socioeconomic systems that are so often the source of their oppression. For example, the kindness of visiting prisoners must be coupled with active concern for humane prison conditions and an equitable judicial system. The kindness of feeding the poor must be coupled with active concern for developing ways to empower them, through education and economic opportunity, so that cycles of poverty are broken. The kindness of caring for the sick must be coupled with active concern for dismantling the social barriers that prevent health education and medical care from reaching the poorest neighborhoods.

Jesus not only served the physical needs of hungry and hurting people, but he also liberated them from and challenged the socioeconomic systems and mindsets that kept them hungry and hurting. Jesus critiqued offering practices, which had become a point of arrogance and pride for some religious persons, and lifted the spirit of a widow woman when he acknowledged the significance of the offering she gave. He said her small offering was greater than the large sums given by others, because the widow gave all she had and left with no financial substance; whereas others gave large sums, but it was out of their abundance; they left with plenty (Mark 12:41-44). He broke cultural tradition by speaking to a Samaritan woman who had come to draw water at midday, thereby liberating her from the social isolation she was used to experiencing. When Jesus spoke to her, he empowered her to fulfill her destiny and she became the first female evangelist for the kingdom of God (John 4:1-42). Jesus wasn't afraid to criticize the hypocritical practices and traditions of the church leaders and politicians of his time. He identified the abusive nature of their traditions, perpetrated by people with clout, and he also drove the money changers out of the temple. He gave sight to the blind, healed broken hearts, and set the captives free. We are to do no less in God's enterprise of mercy.

God's heart breaks over the millions in the world who go to bed hungry and who die of starvation. He also cares about the homeless, the poor, the injured and diseased, the imprisoned, and others who are hurting or disadvantaged. These are people he loves and for whom his Son died. Who is supposed to care for these people? His sheep, the righteous—us! If anyone should be using their wealth and influence in the forefront of the war against world hunger, inhumane treatment, and social injustice, it should be God's people.

Is your motivation for making money purely to give yourself a better lifestyle? Or are you using your abilities to maximize your earning potential in order to meet the needs of hurting people in the world? Those who invest their lives and their substance in alleviating hunger, battling injustice, and serving the needs of others in the world, in loving service to God, are creating eternal wealth. God loves people. Eternal wealth accrues when we love God enough to invest our time and our financial resources in people for whom his heart beats with compassion.

Albert Lexie, a developmentally disabled saint in his sixties, has been shining shoes for a living in Pittsburgh, Pennsylvania, since his teens. He walks to offices and businesses in his neighborhood, giving a good shine for three dollars, and he often receives generous tips.

In 1981 Albert happened to see a Christmas telethon for Children's Hospital of Pittsburgh. They were raising money for their Free Care Fund so children could be treated regardless of their families' financial situation. Albert decided this was a good thing. He donated to the hospital more than seven hundred dollars he had saved from his tips, and he pledged to give all his tips in the future to the hospital's Free Care Fund. Albert also decided to include Children's Hospital in his rounds, despite its distance from his home.

More than two decades later, Albert still gets up early two days a week and takes the bus to Children's Hospital to shine shoes for everyone from surgeons to orderlies. He does this in addition to his regular rounds, which he does on foot. All told, Albert Lexie has donated over one hundred thousand dollars to the Free Care Fund—his tips from more than twenty years of shining shoes. A hospital administrator remarked, "Nobody gives a greater percentage of their income than Albert does."

"Why do you give so much money away?" asked CBS News correspondent Lee Cowan during a television interview.

"Because I love the kids very much. I think they're very special," Albert answered.

"You don't even know them," Cowan said.

"You don't know them, but you still love them," Albert answered. "That's why God put you here."[2]

For each of us, God's mission of mercy is about caring for people in need, from our Jerusalem—the place where we live—to the farthest corners of the world (Acts 1:8). We're not just talking about needy people from one ethnic group, one culture, one skin color, one lifestyle, or one religion. God's heart of compassion is touched when any member of his human creation is suffering. When we are motivated by love to direct our time, energy, and resources into meeting these needs, we not only accrue eternal wealth but we also open opportunities to meet humanity's deepest need through God's mission of grace.

The Mission of Grace

God's compassionate work in the world, the work to which he calls us to invest our energies and resources, goes beyond mercifully meeting physical needs. The Lord also commands us to serve humankind's greatest need: the spiritual poverty of the human soul. If people's physical needs are not met, they may suffer greatly and possibly die. But if their spiritual need for forgiveness of sin and a relationship with God is not met, they will suffer from spiritual emptiness and spend eternity in hell.

God has appointed us to join him in his mission of mercy to save lives and alleviate suffering. God has also appointed us to be part of his mission of grace in the world, sharing the gospel of Jesus as well as helping others grow in their knowledge and understanding of the depth of God's love for us as demonstrated by his grace. Mercy and grace make up God's two-pronged mission for us who serve in his enterprise. And since it is God's enterprise, it is worthy of our investment of the abilities and resources he has given us.

The purpose of God's mission of grace is twofold. First, it is to share with the world the good news of God's salvation and the temporal and eternal benefits of life in his kingdom. Second, it is to empower us to prosper and live an abundant life.

Paul summarized the first aspect of the mission of grace with these words: "The grace of God that brings salvation has appeared to all men. It teaches us to say 'No' to ungodliness and worldly passions, and to live self-controlled, upright and godly lives in this present age, while we wait for the blessed hope—the glorious appearing of our great God and Savior, Jesus Christ, who gave himself for us to redeem us from all wickedness and to purify for himself a people that are his very own, eager to do what is good" (Titus 2:11-14). We are to share the message of God's saving grace with others so they may receive his love and prosper not only physically but also spiritually.

Jesus announced that his Father's mission for him was "to seek and to save what was lost" (Luke 19:10). Later he prayed to his Father regarding his followers, "As you sent me into the world, I have sent them into the world" (John 17:18). Then, in his final words to his disciples, he commissioned them to his mission of grace, also called the Great Commission: "All authority in heaven and on earth has been given to me. Therefore go and make disciples of all nations, baptizing them in the name of the Father and of the Son and of the Holy Spirit, and teaching them to obey everything I have commanded you. And surely I am with you always, to the very end of the age" (Matthew 28:18-20).

God has commissioned us to invite people to become obedient, knowledgeable disciples of Jesus. We carry out this mission as we communicate the truth of the gospel through our words. But the purpose of God's mission of grace doesn't stop there. It is also given to empower us to live victorious lives by laying hold of soul prosperity.

There are different types of grace. There is grace that saves (Ephesians 2:8-9), grace that helps in time of need (Hebrews 4:16), and grace that gives gifts and abilities for service (Ephesians 3:7). There is also grace that equips us, enables us, and empowers us to prosper (Philippians 2:13). When we participate in God's mission of grace, we are charged not only to lead others to the saving knowledge of Jesus but also to personally grow in that knowledge so that our souls will prosper, and we can disciple others and empower them to prosper. And by his grace God provides the resources for us to fulfill this charge.

The Full Scope of God's Mission

Which of God's missions in the world is more important—mercy or grace? The answer to this question is not on one side or the other; it's on both sides. The message of the Bible is certainly about preaching grace and eternal salvation, and it's also about being empowered to prosper, lifting the fallen, healing the hurting, comforting the distressed, and breaking down strongholds of injustice. Jesus came into the world so that we would have access to an abundant life today and life everlasting (John 10:10). He was equally compassionate about alleviating human suffering and dispelling spiritual darkness. He wept over the faithlessness of Jerusalem, and he wept over the grief of his friends Mary and Martha when their brother, Lazarus, died (Luke 19:41-44; John 11:32-35). Mercy and grace are not mutually independent; they are fully integrated and interdependent. The mission of God's enterprise in the world is always both together, ministering to the physical, emotional, and spiritual needs of others simultaneously.

The apostle James, who was Jesus' half brother, made perhaps the most pointed statement in the Bible about the interrelatedness of mercy and grace. He used "works" to describe the enterprise of mercy and "faith" for the grace we have received and share with others.

> What good is it, my brothers, if a man claims to have faith but has no deeds? Can such faith save him? Suppose a brother or sister is without clothes and daily food. If one of you says to him, "Go, I wish you well; keep warm and well fed," but does nothing about his physical needs, what good is it? In the same way, faith by itself, if it is not accompanied by action, is dead.
> But someone will say, "You have faith; I have deeds."
> Show me your faith without deeds, and I will show you my faith by what I do. You believe that there is one God. Good! Even the demons believe that—and shudder....
> As the body without the spirit is dead, so faith without deeds is dead. (James 2:14-19, 26)

Eternal wealth is the reward of those who are fully involved in communicating the message of grace and faith while fully involved in providing the works of both. People are hungry for food, and people are hungry for forgiveness. People are oppressed by unjust socioeconomic systems, and people are oppressed by spiritual darkness. People need good news in their difficult and painful life situations, and they also need to hear the good news of salvation in Christ Jesus. As we serve spiritual needs, we must also serve physical, emotional, and educational needs. Mercy and grace cannot be parceled out separately. God's enterprise is to meet the needs of the people he loves, and the purpose for our prosperity is to make sure it happens.

The full scope of God's enterprise of mercy and grace includes all people everywhere. John 3:16 begins, "God so loved the *world*..." (emphasis added). Christ's commission to his followers was "Go into all the world and preach the good news to all creation" (Mark 16:15). We are to be inclusive, not exclusive, when it comes to distributing our resources in the ministries of mercy and grace. Jesus wants us to be his Spirit-empowered witnesses "in Jerusalem, and in all Judea and Samaria, and to the ends of the earth" (Acts 1:8)—literally, anywhere we find people in need.

> **Our Twofold Mission**
>
> *Mission of mercy:* Meeting the universal human needs for love, food, shelter, safety, respect, kindness, and justice
> *Mission of grace:* Sharing the gospel of Jesus Christ and helping others grow in their understanding of God's love

But notice that our ministry of mercy and grace starts in Jerusalem, right where we live, with those closest to us. This means our first circle of love and caring must be our families—spouse, children, parents, siblings, in-laws, and so on. I believe this was part of the message God was trying to get across to me when he directed me to focus my love on my husband and son. You may feel compelled to prosper so that you can meet the needs of the hungry, the lost, the homeless, and the disenfranchised around the globe. But if you ignore the material, emotional, educational, or spiritual needs of those in your family, you are overlooking God's first priority for your ministry of mercy and grace. Paul minced no words on this subject: "If anyone does not provide for his relatives, and especially for his immediate family, he has denied the faith and is worse than an unbeliever" (1 Timothy 5:8).

So pray earnestly for those in spiritual darkness around the world, but pray first for those related to you who do not know Christ. Give sacrificially to meet the needs of the poor and hungry in your community, but make sure you don't overlook the material, emotional, or educational needs of your spouse and the family members who are closest to you. By all means, support ministries that take the gospel to the four corners of the world, but make sure the light of your witness burns brightly in the lives of those nearest to you. Participating in God's mission of mercy and grace at any level begins at home.

Investing resources in the business of carrying out God's enterprise in the world rarely happens without opposition. Why? Because there is another system for accumulating wealth in our world that clamors for attention and allegiance. I call this kind of wealth *worldly wealth*. It was the allure of worldly wealth, and my entanglement in it, that initially caused me to say no to God when he challenged me to redirect my focus. In the next chapter we will explore how worldly wealth—driven by the prince of this world, the devil—undermines our success at creating eternal wealth.

Questions for Reflection and Discussion

1. There are many ways we can use our skills, abilities, and economic resources to help fulfill God's mission of mercy and grace in the earth. Write down at least three ways you can contribute to the fulfillment of God's mission outside your family.

2. Have you been using your gifts in these ways? Why or why not?

> You cannot serve both God and money.

Chapter 5

The Entanglement of Worldly Wealth

In the months immediately following God's message to me about my priorities, my behavior didn't change. I maintained the same grueling work schedule that had fueled my fast-track rise to success. But something inside my heart was changing. Little by little, my consuming passion for my career began to wane. I could sense my tolerance, patience, and resilience eroding under the pressure of increasing challenges in my work life—challenges that had previously energized me.

I was growing emotionally weary. It became more difficult to maintain the breakneck pace of striving for perfection and working overtime to make things happen. I was tired of being the corporate cheerleader, motivating and inspiring others to dig deeper and give more of themselves to their work and careers. I was tired of dealing with the seemingly endless changes in corporate climate and direction. I was becoming miserable, growing heartsick. Yet I concealed my pain from those around me.

Over a period of several months, my discontentment grew worse and I began to despise my job. Instead of waking up each morning energized and eager to go to work, I dreaded the day ahead. It wasn't just my particular position as division CFO that I hated; there wasn't anything else in the company I wanted to do. Furthermore, I couldn't think of any kind of job with any company that would satisfy me. I didn't want to work for anyone. I wanted to run away from anything that smelled of corporate enterprise. I hated my career!

Approximately one year after I said no to God's clear message to pour my love into my husband and home, I woke up at two o'clock one morning feeling like I was coming out of my skin. I was wracked with anxiety over a terrible dilemma. My career had become a millstone around my neck, pulling me down—to what eventual depths? I wanted out, but I didn't know how I could get out and survive financially. Terence and I had built a very comfortable lifestyle on our combined salaries. There was no way we could maintain our high standard of living without my salary and bonuses. I wanted to quit, but I didn't want to give up the wealth and prestige I had attained. I felt trapped.

My mind racing and emotions churning, I couldn't get back to sleep, so I slipped out of bed and went downstairs. I began to cry out to the Lord in frustration and anger. "Jesus, what's wrong?" I called out, pacing the floor. "I'm wound so tight over this job, I'm ready to explode. You put me in this position. You led me to study accounting and earn my CPA. You gave me great jobs, quick promotions, important responsibilities, and an incredible income. So why am I pacing the floor over my work? I don't like this! It's not the abundant life you promised me. Jesus, please fix it!"

I don't know how long I spent pacing and lashing out at God that night. He listened patiently but did not answer my tearful questions. Looking back, I realize that God had said all he needed to say to me on the issue twelve months earlier: "Julaine, pour your love into your husband and family." I believe God was waiting for me to stop ignoring him and start obeying. In his loving way Jesus was summoning me to participate in God's system of creating eternal wealth. But first he had to help me extricate myself from the system in which I had been entangled all my life—the pursuit of worldly wealth.

As I had deliberately and energetically advanced my career for fourteen years, I was never blind to what I was after. I sought the money, power, and prestige I assumed God wanted me to have. What I was about to discover was that my plan for creating wealth was different from his plan, and my purposes had taken precedence over his purposes. It all came to light when God confronted me in February 2000 and, instead of yielding to him, I said no.

Good Goals, Wrong Motives

Eternal wealth accrues as we invest our life and resources in God's kingdom. A by-product of investing in his kingdom is the overflow of money and material possessions he allows us to use and enjoy along the way. The goal of having nice things is always secondary to God's agenda for what we do. As Jesus said, "Seek first his kingdom and his righteousness"—God's agenda—"and all these things"—the money and things we enjoy and need to live on—"will be given to you as well" (Matthew 6:33). God's agenda in the world is primary; the fruits we may enjoy on the journey are secondary.

I had this equation backward. I was living like the pagans Jesus described in verse 32 who "run after" material things. I was focused on the money, power, and prestige that would support the lifestyle I desired. Focusing on my family and following God's agenda were secondary. I had put the emphasis on doing what I wanted and getting what I wanted, as clearly evidenced by my response when God told me to change my priorities.

Now, creating wealth is something God allows in his kingdom. He even promises us success within the parameters of his kingdom. However, he opposes our pursuit of wealth when we make money and self-centered gain our goal in place of a desire to keep his commandments and to love our neighbors as ourselves. Is God out to spoil our fun? No. He is out to accomplish his purposes in the world through our abilities and resources. To whatever degree we make money and self-centered gain our goal, we impede the achievement of God's purposes for our life.

How are we drawn away from God's purposes for eternal wealth to the selfish purposes of worldly wealth? It occurs when we fall more deeply in love with God's gifts than with God the giver. Jesus said, "You cannot serve both God and Money" (Matthew 6:24). He didn't say we cannot have money; he said we cannot *serve* money and God at the same time. Paul wrote, "The love of money is the root of all kinds of evil" (1 Timothy 6:10). He didn't say money is evil; he said the love of money is evil. Our love is to be directed toward God and people, not money and possessions.

My success in the business world, and all I had gained personally from that success, were gifts to me from God. But I had fallen more in love with these gifts and my self-centered desires than with God and his purposes for me, as proved by my unwillingness to invest my energies in my family as the Lord directed. Somewhere along my pathway to prosperity I began to ignore God's enabling grace, which had given me the ability to create wealth, and I began to exalt my power and will above God's power and will.

We all must respond to God's grace, and there is a right and a wrong response. The wrong response to grace is to "miss it," meaning to fail to acknowledge his grace as our source or power to get wealth. Hebrews 12:15 warns us, "See to it that no one misses the grace of God and that no bitter root grows up to cause trouble and defile many." I began to "miss" God's grace when I considered that it was the strength of my hands, the will of my heart, and the experience and knowledge in my mind alone that brought me wealth. Therefore, I had naively concluded that I could succeed in whatever I wanted to do while disobeying God. I had fallen in love with what I produced, put my confidence entirely in myself, and even began to lose respect for my husband.

The right response to God's grace for creating wealth is to always love the giver more than his gifts. We demonstrate our love for God when we do what he says to do (John 14:15). For me, the right response would have been to acknowledge that God had given me the ability to acquire wealth (Deuteronomy 8:18), to follow his direction, and not to fall into the trap of exalting myself above him by thinking it was my power and the strength of my hands that had produced this wealth for me (verse 17). If God had given me the ability to acquire wealth once, he could do it again.

How can we know if we are more in love with God's gifts than with God himself? I can think of several examples. God puts his finger on something you treasure and says, in effect, "Give it back to me," but you resist or say no. He clearly speaks to you about the career you should pursue, but you'd rather do something else because you're convinced you'll be able to earn more money or prestige that way. You know God is directing you to spend more time with your kids or spouse, but you have to put in more overtime to remain in the running for a big promotion and raise, so you continue to make family time a low priority.

When having or seeking things prevents you from obeying God and using them as the he directs, you have missed God's grace and you are creating worldly wealth instead of eternal wealth. Making worldly wealth your priority is wrong because it demotes God from his rightful place of supremacy in all things (see Colossians 1:18).

In the book of Revelation, the kingdom of Babylon is the picture God uses to describe the world's system for acquiring economic prosperity, managing wealth, and living in luxury apart from him (see Revelation 18). A heavenly being proclaims, "Fallen! Fallen is Babylon the Great! She has become a home for demons and a haunt for every evil spirit, a haunt for every unclean and detestable bird. For all the nations have drunk the maddening wine of her adulteries. The kings of the earth committed adultery with her, and the merchants of the earth grew rich from her excessive luxuries" (verses 2-3). Then God commands his people to separate themselves from the world's system for creating and managing wealth. "Come out of [Babylon], my people, so that you will not share in her sins, so that you will not receive any of her plagues; for her sins are piled up to heaven, and God has remembered her crimes" (verses 4-5).

What does it mean to live in Babylon when it comes to creating wealth? Here are seven behaviors that I believe reveal misplaced priorities for acquiring and managing our wealth and that characterize life in Babylon. They are the telltale signs of the pursuit of worldly wealth.

1. Trusting in the world's system and financial indicators for creating and managing wealth more than trusting in God.

The world's system says the more money you accumulate, keep, and invest for yourself, the more you'll have. No doubt saving, investing, and building wealth through investments made per the advice of financial planners, stockbrokers, bankers, and other professionals in the financial industry can help us acquire and manage financial resources. And there are countless books, seminars, Web sites, and other tools out there designed to equip us for making wise financial decisions. You should check market trends and projections and consult knowledgeable sources before making financial decisions. But danger lies in basing your decisions on the world's standards and financial indicators without consulting God's "indicators" and following the principles for financial increase found in his Word. If we only invest in ourselves, and if we trust in experts and money more than we trust in

God and his Word, our return will benefit us and others only in this life and not for eternity.

2. *Relying on past experiences for career and financial decision making more than direction received today through prayer.*

Maybe last week—or last month or last year—you sensed God's direction to earn, give, spend, save, or invest in a certain way. Basing career and financial decisions on past experiences or successes only, instead of seeking God's wisdom and direction for today through a lifestyle of prayer, will draw you away from him. God stands willing to empower us and direct us in the use of our abilities and resources. If we fail to seek his help in prayer, however, we limit what the Lord can do in us and through us.

3. *Trusting in our abilities and the help of others alone to increase wealth.*

God has given us gifts and abilities, as well as the help of other people, for creating wealth. A big mistake many people make is trusting in those abilities exclusively, without acknowledging the role God's grace plays in our ability to increase financially. If we ignore the grace he gives us to create wealth, we will separate God from our income-producing efforts. "God opposes the proud but gives grace to the humble" (James 4:6). The most humbling thing we can do is to admit that we need God and to demonstrate our humility when we pray. When we acknowledge the role his grace plays in our ability to create wealth, we always pray about and follow his direction for our career and finances.

4. *Making decisions to please others instead of God.*

Some people are so dependent on the approval of others that this even determines how they acquire and manage their material resources. They will take a job their spouse or parent wants them to have. They will give to a charity or ministry because others do. They will invest in a mutual fund solely because a parent or friend recommended it. The counsel and encouragement of others is good, but not as the sole basis for career and financial decisions. Always ask God first and seek to please him

5. Regarding material prosperity as the prime indicator of personal success and God's blessing.

The world's system judges people's success based on how much wealth and fame they have. Lifestyles of the rich and famous are exalted as the standard for success in the world, and unless you measure up, you're not considered important. People who are wealthy are assumed to be blessed, whereas people who are not are thought to be relatively unsuccessful and, perhaps even worse, cursed. In God's kingdom, however, the standard for personal success and God's blessing is not your net worth in dollars. It is the condition of your relationship with God and your faithfulness in serving him with all you have. Don't fall into the trap of using your net worth as a measure of your personal success or God's blessing, because it is possible to be rich in things and poor in the things of God that produce eternal wealth.

6. Pursuing wealth and possessions on our own terms.

In the parable of the three servants, the third servant was rebuked for failing to follow the master's instructions to invest his talent of gold and produce a return for his master. Our efforts to create wealth by doing what we think is best, buying into a consumer-oriented mentality, and seeking to accumulate things while ignoring God's agenda will prove just as fruitless.

Wrong Goals, Grave Dangers

There's another reason God calls us away from Babylon and the pursuit of worldly wealth. It is a dangerous way to live, and God doesn't want us to get hurt. Here are some of the dangers associated with worldly wealth that we are warned against in Scripture.

1. The danger of a self-indulgent life.
"Now listen, you rich people. You have lived on earth in luxury and self-indulgence. You have fattened yourself in the day of slaughter" (James 5:1, 5). Being self-indulgent is taking unrestrained pleasure for oneself to the point of gratifying every desire. Those who seek wealth only to indulge themselves without limit are like fattened animals headed for slaughter. Better to invest our wealth in the enterprise that will transcend time.

2. The danger of an uncertain future.
"Command those who are rich in this present world not to be arrogant nor to put their hope in wealth, which is so uncertain, but to put their hope in God, who richly provides us with everything for our enjoyment" (1 Timothy 6:17). The material wealth God allows us to create is transitory and temporal, subject to such uncertainties as stock market failure, business failure, and other calamities that can wipe out a financial portfolio overnight. Put your trust in the eternally certain Giver, not in his gifts.

3. The danger of unfruitful motives.
"You want something but don't get it. You kill and covet, but you cannot have what you want. You quarrel and fight. You do not have, because you do not ask God. When you ask, you do not receive, because you ask with wrong motives, that you may spend what you get on your pleasures" (James 4:2-3). Those who focus on God's gifts instead of on God himself pray selfish prayers. They want more, more, more for themselves. God is not compelled to answer prayers that exclude God and his agenda.

4. The danger of choosing the wrong master.

"No one can serve two masters. Either he will hate the one and love the other, or he will be devoted to the one and despise the other. You cannot serve both God and Money" (Matthew 6:24). If we devote our lives to financial and material prosperity, we are not serving God. If we try to appease our appetite for wealth while maintaining allegiance to God, we are not serving God. And by choosing the wrong master, we limit our wealth to what money can buy for us, which excludes everything of eternal value.

5. The danger of oppressing others.

"Now listen, you rich people, weep and wail because of the misery that is coming upon you.... You have hoarded wealth in the last days. Look! The wages you failed to pay the workmen who mowed your fields are crying out against you. The cries of the harvesters have reached the ears of the Lord Almighty" (James 5:1, 3-4). The rich people in this passage were so self-indulgent that they spent money that belonged to their employees on themselves. Being more in love with God's material gifts than with God will prompt us to earn and spend selfishly and exploit people instead of giving generously to others.

6. The danger of personal ruin.

"People who want to get rich fall into temptation and a trap and into many foolish and harmful desires that plunge men into ruin and destruction" (1 Timothy 6:9). Striving for wealth without accountability to God can unleash many harmful appetites and ruinous addictions.

7. The danger of wandering from the faith.

"The love of money is a root of all kinds of evil. Some people, eager for money, have wandered from the faith and pierced themselves with many griefs" (1 Timothy 6:10). Following hard after wealth for personal gain and pleasure can draw us far from the path of righteousness in the service of Jesus. The farther we wander from God's ways, the more hurtful and destructive it will be to us.

8. *The danger of idolatry.*
"Some pour out gold from their bags and weigh out silver on the scales; they hire a goldsmith to make it into a god, and they bow down and worship it" (Isaiah 46:6). Few people in Western culture bow down to a graven image as people did in biblical times and still do in some other cultures today. The idols we worship are usually material goods (house, car, boat, bank account), people (spouse, child, famous person, illicit lover), experiences (sex, leisure activities, work), and ideologies (democracy, religious traditions, values). No matter what the object, idolatry is idolatry, and God says worshiping anything or anyone but him is abominable.

9. *The danger of ultimate destruction.*
"If you ever forget the LORD your God and follow other gods and worship and bow down to them, I testify against you today that you will surely be destroyed" (Deuteronomy 8:19). The ultimate payoff of cherishing God's gifts above worshiping him as the giver is something no one wants: destruction. An eternity in hell is the destination of all who "worshiped and served created things rather than the Creator" (Romans 1:25). No one should want to get anywhere near that path and its negative consequences.

Deliverance in the Face of Danger
As a vice president at AT&T Broadband, my mantra was "Leaders never have a bad day." In the weeks following my middle-of-the-night confrontation with God, I kept reciting it, trying to convince myself that it was true and to hide my negative attitude from my staff and colleagues. I thought I was doing a pretty good job of fronting and managing my day-to-day

activities. Then one afternoon my boss hit me between the eyes with a simple but perceptive question.

"Julaine, what's wrong with you?" LeAnn asked.

"Nothing," I replied quickly.

"Are you sure?"

At that moment the Lord spoke into my spirit. "Tell her the truth." I hesitated, and God said it again: "Tell her the truth! Do it!"

The words caught in my throat and time seemed to stand still. I didn't know what would happen if I answered her truthfully. How could I reveal to my superior something so personal and potentially destructive to my career? But in that moment I knew freedom was near after months of inner turmoil.

"I hate my job," I said to my boss. At that moment I sensed both jubilation at having finally confessed my torment and great fear at knowing I had probably sealed my fate with the company. Emotions welled up inside me, and the floodgates of my heart burst open with tears. It was the emotional release I had blocked for many months. I was free.

Once I had regained control of my emotions, LeAnn said, "I've been watching you, Julaine, and I can see that you are unhappy. Life is too short to be miserable at work. What do you want to do?"

Relieved at LeAnn's sympathy and concern, I felt free to open my heart. "I really want to quit, but I'm not in a financial position to do it."

After some discussion, LeAnn sensed that I was sincere about my decision to leave. She offered to support me in whatever decision I made. I was blown away by her kindness and helpfulness. Having unburdened my heart and been blessed by LeAnn's support, I finally knew what to do. That very day I resigned my once-coveted position at AT&T Broadband.

Then I had to tell my husband what I had done, and I wasn't eager to do so. Our move from San Francisco to Seattle only two years earlier had required that Terence make a job transfer. He had gone through all the difficulties of a big family transition and put his career in jeopardy so I could pursue my dream at AT&T. Now I was tossing my career overboard. A man of quiet strength and few words, Terence seemed to take the news in stride. It would be much later before we sorted through the many ramifications of my decision for our marriage and family life, including the fear and sense of betrayal it sparked in my husband.

The company and I negotiated my exit, and two months later I walked away from what I regarded as the best career I would ever have and the most money I would ever earn. I was no longer a vice president, CFO, or finance officer. I was nothing. I didn't have a job and I didn't want a job. There were no more projects or promotions to compete for, no more dreams of a position higher up the corporate ladder. I wanted none of it.

I felt confident that I was following the Spirit's leading, but I was also scared to death. I was saying goodbye to financial security and walking into the insecurity of an unknown future. Not long after that pivotal conversation with my boss, I found myself prostrate on my kitchen floor, crying out to God. "What have I done?" I wailed. "How could I be so stupid and weak as to throw away my career just because of a little job discontent? How will I make up for the income void I created by refusing to persevere?"

My mind was terrorized by thoughts of failure and impending financial ruin. It was an ungodly fear based on unbelief, a fear that I would lose everything I had and never have everything I wanted. It's a fear that stalks many of us when our earthly source of financial security disappears. Two weeks following my decision, my fears had me pinned to the kitchen floor in tears. It seemed that my life was over.

Then I heard God say to me, "Get up, Julaine. Your life isn't over. In fact, I have saved the best for last." It was the beginning of my deliverance from captivity in Babylon.

Questions for Reflection and Discussion

1. In the book of Galatians, Paul asks us a question: "After beginning with the Spirit, are you now trying to attain your goal by human effort?" Often we begin our career journey listening closely to God and responding in a right manner to his grace. However, as we experience the joy of success, and as our confidence in our skills and abilities increase, we try to finish what we started through human effort. We miss God's grace and wind up in Babylonian captivity. In what ways has your response to career success, your relationship with money, or your pursuit of financial prosperity demonstrated that you are ensnared in Babylon captivity?

2. What habits or attitudes toward money and/or your career do you feel God wants to change in your life?

" In God's economy,

business and financial activities

are platforms for expressing love. "

Chapter 6

THE INVISIBLE HAND

When I heard God say to me, "I have saved the best for last," it gave me a boost of hope. But, frankly, I had my doubts that much good—let alone the best—could come from saying goodbye to my job. To me, giving up my CPA career was the same thing as kissing my money goodbye. How could "the best" come from giving away my earning power?

Only later did I realize that God was out to challenge what I believed about how to make and manage money. But at the time I was convinced that money, the good life it could buy, and my CPA career were inseparable; I couldn't have one without the others. That day on the kitchen floor when realization of the consequences of my actions hit me hard, God confronted me with the choice everyone must face if they desire to create eternal wealth: was I going to put my trust in him or money for the things I needed and desired? Jesus made it clear that we can't do both (see Matthew 6:24).

While I wanted to believe that God would miraculously supply all my needs and give me the desires of my heart, the truth was that my hope for financial success and satisfaction of my interests was deeply ingrained in trust in my earning power, not in God's power. I was primarily looking to my job and my paycheck to supply everything I needed and wanted in this world. As I began life after my successful career, the Lord was asking me to transform my thinking to seek him first and let him supply my needs and wants.

My dilemma illustrates the tension between two ways to achieve financial prosperity that spring from two core beliefs about money and wealth. One belief exalts money and is self-centered. It motivates people to view money as their security and means of satisfying self-interest. That's where I was living before God brought me up short. The other belief sees money as a tool and is God-centered. It motivates people to seek God and to relate to money based on his guidance and a desire to satisfy his interests. This was the "best" God was talking to me about. In order to create eternal wealth, our relationship with money and wealth must be guided by the hand of God instead of the hand of self-interest.

The Invisible Hand of Self-Interest

In 1776, Scottish economist and philosopher Adam Smith, who is considered the father of modern-day economic theory, coined the phrase "the invisible hand." According to Smith, the satisfaction of individual self-interest is the invisible hand, or motivating factor, that efficiently and effectively distributes wealth within a society. In his book *The Wealth of Nations*, Smith states:

> Man has almost constant occasion for the help of his brethren, and it is in vain for him to expect it from their benevolence only. He will be more likely to prevail if he can interest their self-love in his favour, and show them that it is for their own advantage to do for him what he requires of them. Whoever offers to another a bargain of any kind, proposes to do this: Give me that which I want, and you shall have this which you want, is the meaning of every such

offer; and it is in this manner that we obtain from one another the far greater part of those good offices which we stand in need of.[1]

In other words, people relate to one another in whatever way gains them what they want and need. And since, according to Smith, everyone operates this way, the wealth of the world flows from hand to hand as people work the angles to get what they need in exchange for what others need. For example, a storeowner may make greater profit by selling an abundance of products at a discount than fewer products at full retail. Why? Because the consumer gets what he wants by paying less and is willing to buy more, so both seller and buyer get what they want.

When the motivation of an economic system is wealth creation and satisfaction of self-interest, any consideration of the interests of others or benevolence to others is no more than a by-product. Generosity and philanthropy are always secondary to personal profit under the invisible hand of self-interest.

Self-interest drives people to work hard and earn as much money as they can so they can meet their financial and material needs and desires. Self-interest also drives other endeavors to acquire money. For example, Americans spend billions of dollars annually on lottery tickets, hoping to hit the winning numbers so they can have everything they want. And, of course, covetousness, greed, and self-interest are at the root of most crime. People want money and material goods so badly that they will do whatever it takes to get them—steal, deal drugs, commit fraud, and even kill.

For the person who exalts money and is guided by a desire to satisfy self-interest, life is often marked by fear, envy, greed, and anxiety. When money is the source of your satisfaction, you can never have enough. You will live in fear that your needs will not be met. You will chase after money and compromise your convictions, values, and integrity to get it. You will view others with envy because they have things you don't. You will make decisions based on greed and envy.

When you believe that money is the source of your satisfaction, your sense of self-worth will be based on the things you own. Money will become a source of arguments between you and those you love. You will ignore the material needs of others because their lack emphasizes your wealth and because you are bent on accumulating wealth instead of distributing it. You will miss out on many opportunities in life because you will constantly be chasing after more money. Ironically, achieving satisfaction by acquiring money and possessions for yourself is fruitless because self-centeredness always craves more, more, more.

The prevailing traditions, habits, myths, and assumptions in culture tend to drive our behaviors. And the most powerful drivers in the money-loving world in which we live insist that increasing wealth results in increasing happiness and that the only way to increase wealth is to make acquiring money our top priority. After more than two centuries, Adam Smith's invisible hand of self-interest is still the guiding hand in world economics.

The Invisible Hand of God

Amazingly, many Christians are pushed along through life by Adam Smith's invisible hand of self-interest when it comes to money and wealth. Why? Because they lack an understanding of the principles of God's economy and fall back on the world's principles by default. They are unaware that Adam Smith's invisible hand is not the only motivating factor for hard work and wealth accumulation. God also has an "invisible hand" when it comes to money and wealth in the form of what he reveals to us in his Word about his desires and our motives for making and spending money. And God's invisible hand regarding money and wealth is 100 percent reliable because it is consistent with his eternal truth, not faulty human tradition, habit, myth, or assumption.

The foundation for God's economy is Matthew 6:33: "Seek first his kingdom and his righteousness, and all these things will be given to you as well." From God's perspective, seeking him must take precedence over seeking anything else. It should be the motivating factor behind the work we do. Contrary to the world's economic system, the way to satisfy our material needs and desires in God's economy is to focus our lives on God, understand his will, and satisfy his plans. In the process of our seeking him first, God promises to meet all our needs and the desires of our hearts, which means he will put us to work on the tasks that will generate results meeting our needs and fulfilling our desires. If we fail to believe God's promise, we will fail to focus our attention on doing what he wants us to do, fail to discover our destiny, and fail to relate to our money and possessions the way we should. And to whatever extent we fail to discover our destiny and instead relate to our wealth improperly, we risk forfeiting the eternal purposes of God and the wealth he promises us.

In the process of seeking God first, our self-interests are also satisfied. How can this be? That's the question I tearfully asked God while lying on the kitchen floor after deciding to leave my job. I couldn't see how I could get what I wanted by giving up my career. I had yet to learn that seeking God is a goal, a long-term point of focus that establishes direction for short-term performance. That means that while your short-term steps may not appear to be taking you in the direction where you want to go, as long as you focus on seeking God, he will guide you to your destination. When you seek God first, your mind is set so that the steps you take from the decisions you make lead you closer to the place he wants you to be. And the closer you get to the place God wants you to be, the closer you get to his provisions.

Changing our motivating factor for making money from self first to God first is part of the transformation of becoming a new creation in Christ (2 Corinthians 5:17). As a new creation, we begin to believe, think, speak, and act differently toward money than we did before we gave our life to God. Ezekiel 11:19 says that our old, stony heart becomes a new heart of flesh, a heart that is pliable and accepting of God's ways. God puts new desires—his desires—in our heart so he can give us the desires of our heart.

As long as we seek God first in all things, our economic choices won't be guided solely by Adam Smith's invisible hand. They will also be guided by God's invisible hand, which compels us to consider others as well as ourselves in the use of our money and possessions. Smith claimed that we do consider others, but only as a means of getting what we want from them. That's not the mindset of the new creation in God's economy. As we seek God first, our primary focus is his mission of meeting our spiritual and material needs so that we can help meet the needs of people, not for what we get in return from them but because our focus on others opens the door for God to meet our needs.

Love in God's Economy

In some ways God's economy operates just like the world's economy. People divide their labor and specialize. Earning money is a way to obtain purchasing power, and purchasing power is used to buy the goods and services you desire but cannot produce yourself. Your ability to earn money is based on your ability to earn wages, accrue interest and dividends, sell products or services, collect rental income, and so on. And in God's economy you can become financially wealthy just as in the world's economy. But there are several ways in which God's economy differs from the world's economy. And the biggest difference has to do with love.

In God's economy, it is our love for the Lord, demonstrated by a desire to please him and to satisfy his interests, and not greed, covetousness, and the satisfaction of individual self-interest, that motivates us to transact business in the marketplace. The first and second greatest commandments drive marketplace decisions in God's economic system: love the Lord with all your heart, soul, mind, and strength, and love your neighbor as yourself (Matthew 22:37-39). As we seek God first by following these commandments, we look for opportunities to satisfy God's interests as we transact business to meet our needs and the needs of others. In God's economy our business and financial activities become a platform for expressing love for God and others.

Our wealth is still made in the world's system, and so we must compete in the same marketplace the world competes in. While we transact business motivated by love, we also must be shrewd as serpents and innocent as doves (Matthew 10:16). We must know how to fight the good economic fight: negotiate, lead, make decisions, apply information, analyze facts and trends, keep emotions in check, get up when knocked down, and not take no for an answer. We must be motivated by love and operate with the spirit of the Lion of the tribe of Judah (Revelation 5:5)!

If our business and financial activities are supposed to be a platform for expressing love for God and others, does that mean our self-interests are never fulfilled? For example, must we abandon our desire for a better car or nicer house because there are always people whose need for a better car or nicer house is greater than ours? Or must we abandon our desire to make huge profits because there are corrupt and ruthless people who pursue financial gain through illegal or immoral means? Must we shy away from gaining influence at work or in our community because there are people who abuse power? No, I'm not saying that, nor do I believe God is saying that.

Remember, the second greatest commandment Jesus gave is that we love our neighbors as ourselves (Matthew 22:39). Proper self-love is important to God. Proving what is the acceptable will of God for us by maximizing our earning potential and positively impacting the world we live in is a good thing. God wants our needs to be met as much as he wants the needs of others to be met, and the Bible promises that God will meet our needs and give us the desires of our heart (Psalm 37:4; Philippians 4:19).

We may make a profit, own a nicer house, or fulfill any other legitimate need or desire as long as our acquisition of these things results because we seek God first and does not come at the expense of our obedience to him. This simply means that in our pursuits we give God the option of directing our resources elsewhere. In other words, if, as you're shopping for a new house or car or outfit or toy, you sense God directing you to invest your money elsewhere, then you willingly—even joyfully—set your pursuit aside to do what he says. Or as you are planning how to invest money in your business, if you sense God directing you to defer the investment and instead give an offering to your church, then you willingly—even joyfully—do what he says.

In God's economy love for God and people compels us to give to others without expecting to receive anything from them in return. In God's economy the needs of the poor and disenfranchised are given consideration when economic decisions are made. This means that the more God enables us to create wealth, the greater our responsibility to serve the needs of others. We may also be asked to give to persons or organizations that have more than we do. God does not discriminate and neither should we. Everything we gain belongs to God, so we must pass along to others whatever he asks us to give.

Profit in God's Economy

In God's economy purchasing power is just as important as in the world's economy. After all, God's enterprise is worldwide, and the needs of the world are great. God isn't poor, just scraping along to make ends meet. His economy isn't broken down, powerless, or poverty-stricken. Jesus is God of the universe and everything belongs to him. Jesus has placed everything at our disposal so that we may prosper and control purchasing power under his lordship. We distribute from our wealth to meet the needs of a hurting world.

Prudent management of resources and power increases our favor among people. Hard work earns increasing pay. Wise saving and investing earn interest and dividends. Shrewd buying and selling garner a profit. Careful financial planning and spending allow for more discretionary income at the end of the month. As God's people operate within the world's economic system, while devoted to seeking him above satisfying self-interest, there will be more than enough purchasing power in God's kingdom to fund his enterprise. God's people will produce what they can in abundance so that others will benefit from their labors. And in the process God's people will enjoy the surplus of their God-honoring financial efforts.

By 2001, I'd come a long way from my youthful idea that God wanted me to be poor financially. Today I am convinced that God's plan for each of us includes financial prosperity. The degree of financial prosperity we achieve is contingent upon the resources available to us and our skills, abilities, and attitude in response to God's wealth-creating grace. We must make and spend money in compliance with the core values God has laid down in his Word for his enterprise in the world. Our purposes for prosperity must align with God's purposes. Only by following his principles for creating wealth can we avoid Babylonian captivity and the temptation to create worldly wealth. Only by creating wealth God's way will we enjoy the fruit of our labor for eternity.

When we seek first the kingdom of God and his righteousness, our relationship with money turns from being based on greed, covetousness, and the satisfaction of self-interest to viewing money as an instrument for demonstrating love in three dimensions: love for God, love for self, and love for others.

I ended a fourteen-year CPA career literally lying on my kitchen floor, hoping that somehow God would lift me up again and that I would find fulfillment in life. I began a new journey, not knowing where it would take me. The journey to finding God's next "job" for me took four years and included times of loneliness, fear, and anxiety. There were moments of great faith as well as periods of great doubt and uncertainty. I didn't know whether I would ever see days of prosperity and financial success again. But on the journey I did learn the foundational principles for creating eternal wealth and about profitable living in God's economy. Armed with these principles and truths, it was time to get back into the money making game.

I was no longer worried about whether I would run the right race. I was convinced that God would once again guide my career to just the right place for me as he did when he first directed me to study accounting and become a CPA. I wasn't exactly sure where I was headed but I was willing to pursue God until I found out. I was not going to let pride and arrogance cause me to miss the call he had on my life.

During the years that followed, I discovered God had a plan for me that fit my desire to be a successful businessperson into the bigger scheme of his kingdom. I discovered that God's Word is full of guidance for how to succeed in the marketplace. All I had to do was stop assuming that the Scriptures were only relevant to my spiritual development, and then I began to see the depth of wisdom they contained for building leadership, money-management, and business skills. I also discovered, and participated first-hand, in God's purpose-defining, vision-producing process. This process was the key that unlocked my understanding of my purpose in God's kingdom and propelled me to action for creating eternal wealth. The things I learned are detailed in part 2.

Creating eternal wealth is not a get-rich-quick scheme. We have to apply ourselves to developing skills and abilities that form the basis upon which money is made and wealth is created in the world's system. Christians who have made lots of money know something that Christians who live from paycheck to paycheck or barely make ends meet don't: it takes more than faith to make and manage money. In part 2 I will identify and explain the practical strategies for developing and applying God's plan for creating eternal wealth within the world's system. And we'll take a look at the attributes and skills that must be added to faith to make and manage money so we can create eternal wealth.

Questions for Reflection and Discussion

1. In what ways is God challenging your beliefs about wealth and how you relate to money?

2. Do you believe it's possible to have a relationship with money based on love for God, instead of greed and self-satisfaction, and be able to create wealth? Why or why not?

3. In what ways can spending decisions show that your motives for acquiring wealth are based on love and not a desire for self-satisfaction?

PART 2

CREATING ETERNAL WEALTH

> Vision that creates eternal wealth is birthed from your purpose.

Chapter 7

DISCOVERING YOUR PURPOSE FOR ETERNAL WEALTH

The idea that we can somehow make our money last forever may be difficult for some people to take in at first. That's because being able to embrace the principles for creating eternal wealth requires a change in mindset. The idea of eternal wealth stands on a way of thinking about money that gives preeminence to our relationship with God. Most people give preeminence to their relationship with money in their marketplace endeavors. What lies at the heart of creating eternal wealth, however, is a desire to fulfill God's purpose for our life that is based on a vision for what he can do with our money— a vision greater than what we could conceive on our own. Armed with this vision, we are able to pursue our careers with the courage, focus, optimism, and confidence that empower us to become marketplace leaders who lead with inspiration and conviction while standing for righteousness and justice.

Whether our skills and abilities enable us to run a multibillion-dollar corporation or to work as a mail-room clerk, there are no insignificant people or assignments in God's kingdom. However, of him to whom much is given, much is required. Therefore, the greater the level of gifts and abilities we're given, the greater degree of responsibility and impact we are expected to have when we employ ourselves in the marketplace for the sake of God's kingdom. But each person can make an impact. In God's kingdom, people with relatively lower levels of abilities are also expected to maximize their potential for creating eternal wealth. Guided by purpose and inspired by our conviction in that purpose, we each can turn business, politics, ministry, or any other area of work into vehicles through which we positively impact the families we love and the communities we serve for the sake of the kingdom of God.

Recall that the third servant in the parable we read earlier, who, relatively speaking, wasn't as rich in money or ability as the other servants, was nonetheless given the same opportunity to create wealth and was expected to create wealth for his master. Instead of doing what he could with what he was given, he chose to waste it. Like so many people who believe the little they can do won't make a difference, he failed to recognize that what is never attempted will never be accomplished. Even the smallest of efforts defeats doing nothing at all.

Do you believe that?

A man was walking along the beach when he noticed a young girl throwing something into the water. As he approached her, he saw that the objects she was throwing in the water were starfish. The girl was surrounded by them. For miles and miles, all over the shoreline of the beach, there seemed to be millions of them. "Why would you waste your time throwing the starfish into the water?" he asked the young girl.

She looked up as she grabbed another starfish and answered, "If these starfish are on the beach in the morning, when the tide goes out they will die."

"But that's ridiculous!" cried the man. "Look around you. There are thousands of miles of beach and millions of starfish. How can you possibly think that what you're doing is going to make a difference?"

The young girl picked up another starfish, paused thoughtfully, and then answered as she tossed it out into the sea, "It makes a difference to this one."[1]

People who create eternal wealth in God's kingdom make a difference, regardless of how much or how little money, talent, or ability they start out with, because creating eternal wealth is a matter of using our money and talents to fulfill God's plans. And God doesn't make any insignificant people or plans. Having crossed the pathway that divides the creation of worldly wealth from the pathway to eternal wealth, I'm now fully convinced that not participating in God's plan for the use of the resources we steward is not an option. He expects us to make an attempt to maximize our potential for his kingdom's sake. Indeed, if we fail to act, or if we act without understanding, we open the door to perils of life.

Imagine what your neighborhood will be like ten years from now if people with God-inspired purpose who have the capabilities to live productive lives and create eternal wealth either choose to do nothing with their potential or else stay so trapped by their circumstances that they fail to get out of their underperforming mentality. Imagine for a moment what the future will be like if, while the ones who carry God's vision for creating eternal wealth do nothing, people of power and influence around the world who don't love or fear God continue to value money more than people. Imagine what your community will be like ten, twenty, or thirty years from now if people who control the financial markets in our global economy continue to value things and profit more than people and families. Imagine what your day of accountability with the Master will be like when you have to answer the question, "What did you do with the resources I gave you?"

The challenges are complex and the issues are deep. Nevertheless, if we want to create eternal wealth, our vision for how money should be used in our personal life must align with our God-given purpose and his standards as presented to us from Genesis to Revelation.

As each of us grabs hold of God's purpose for the use of our life and resources on a personal level and do what we can to create eternal wealth, it will impact how money is made and used on a global level. The world needs a new vision for the purpose of prosperity, and that vision comes from God. God always gives his vision to the church. Therefore, the church—the called-out ones—must grab hold of a purpose and a vision for creating eternal wealth.

The Pathway to Purpose and Divine Vision

The most important step to appropriating what we need in order to maximize our potential to create and manage eternal wealth is gaining an understanding of our purpose and conceiving divine vision for our prosperity. Purpose is the original intent of a thing. When God made us, he did so with a specific purpose in mind. That purpose includes a plan for the use of our gifts, talents, and resources. Therefore, if we want to know our purpose and see God's plan for our prosperity, we have to ask him. That means prayer.

Many people think their purpose originates from personal passion. But while your passion can be an indicator of your purpose, the reverse relationship is actually true. Purpose produces passion. Passion is fuel, in the form of desire, compelling you to act in a manner that leads to the fulfillment of your vision, which is generated by a purpose. That purpose comes from God, and prayer opens the door to discovering your purpose. Understanding purpose produces vision. And vision generates the fuel—passion— for seeing God's will fulfilled in your life.

Let me show you how all this can work.

Before I fully surrendered myself to God's perfecting process, I got an idea for a new business. And since I was unemployed, I thought it would be an excellent way to supplement our family's income. I love going to day spas for luxurious manicures, pedicures, facials, massages, and so on. One day it occurred to me, *Why not turn what I love into a business?* Just like that, I made a decision: I was going to open a day spa that rivaled the best spas in the Pacific Northwest!

Kicking my business skills into gear, I formulated a plan. I studied the day-spa industry, researched the Northwest marketplace, and hired an attorney to incorporate my business. I had several major needs: a business partner (since I didn't know anything about running a day spa), a location, employees, and financial backing. I also needed God's blessing. So after I decided what I was going to do and how I was going to do it, I started to pray and ask God to bless my vision. My prayer life was hit-and-miss at that time, but when I did pray, I put the things I needed for my new business at the top of my prayer list.

I even quoted Scripture passages to remind God of how serious I was. One of them was Psalm 37:5-6: "Commit your way to the LORD; trust in him and he will do this: he will make your righteousness shine like the dawn, the justice of your cause like the noonday sun." By asking for his help, I just knew I would succeed. This was my way of integrating my faith and my work. I had made the plans, and now I expected God to bless them so that I would prosper.

It was during this time that the Lord began to say to me, "Julaine, I want you to get up every morning at six o'clock to pray." Now, I was in no mood either to get up or to pray at six in the morning. I didn't have a job, so I loved sleeping late in the mornings. Furthermore, as a goal-oriented, get-things-done kind of person, I considered praying to be unproductive—especially at the crack of dawn! So I continued to sleep in.

This went on for several weeks as I kept working on my plan for the spa. God kept nudging me to get up early for prayer, and I kept sleeping in. Then one morning he said, "Julaine, if Leo asked you to be in his office at 6:00 AM, you would do it. You would even arrive early, well dressed, makeup on, hair combed, anticipating the subject of the meeting. Now *I'm calling you to a meeting. Get up early and pray!*"

Leo had been my boss for seven years, and God had used him to bless me financially in several ways. God's stern point was clear. I would get up early to receive direction from Leo because meeting with Leo might bring a financial benefit. But I wouldn't get up to hear from God. I had linked financial prosperity to my relationship with a rich and powerful businessman more than to the God who had made both me and Leo. The way God confronted me that day filled me with holy fear. The Lord left no doubt in my mind that he expected me to meet with him because he had instructions about my life after AT&T. From that day on, I had no problem rising early to pray.

One morning, just before arising for one of my six o'clock prayer times, the Lord directed me to read from Jeremiah 2. I had no idea what the chapter was about, but I knew Jeremiah's prophecies were not always pleasant. God had just pruned away my career and big salary, so I wasn't in the mood for a word of correction. I wanted to read something encouraging, but I didn't think I would find it in Jeremiah 2.

Starting at verse 1, I didn't see anything that applied to me. But when I reached verse 13, the words leaped out at me: "My people have committed two sins: They have forsaken me, the spring of living water, and have dug their own cisterns, broken cisterns that cannot hold water." I sensed God had something to say to me about sins and cisterns. I didn't like where this was headed, but I kept reading.

When I got to verses 36 and 37, the words sank into my heart: "Why do you go about so much, changing your ways? You will be disappointed by Egypt as you were by Assyria. You will also leave that place with your hands on your head, for the LORD has rejected those you trust; you will not be helped by them."

Then I heard God telling me what was on his mind. "You have built your own cistern. You have made your own plans to create a source of financial security. You didn't ask me for a plan; you devised your own plan and asked me to bless it. You're going to be disappointed with your plan, because I'm not going to honor it."

I knew the Lord was talking about the day-spa business. In my haste to find fulfillment as an entrepreneur after leaving AT&T, and to hold on to something from the past while trying to create something of substance for my future, I had relied totally on my experience and selfish desires as I planned my new business. I hadn't sought God's counsel before making my decision. I only tried to gain his involvement, blessing, favor, and supernatural resources to ensure my success. The Lord firmly let me know that he wasn't interested in blessing my prideful and self-centered behavior.

My decision to open a day spa was based on the flimsiest of reasons: because I liked going to day spas. I had figured out what I wanted to do and did it. It was all pride, arrogance, and selfish ambition, fueled by passion, without prayer. From a business standpoint, I was doing all the right things to get a new venture off the ground. But I had failed to seek God first to find out if it was what he wanted me to do. It's how I had run my life for the past two years. No wonder God was so direct about calling me to prayer at 6:00 AM to receive his direction.

I knew I had to cancel my plan for a day spa. I didn't want to, but I did it anyway because God wasn't in it. Then I had to do something that is very hard for me: nothing. I had no job, and I had released my ambitious business plan, so for the first time in fourteen years I had nothing to do. Every morning my husband went off to work, and our son went off to school, and I was left at home feeling unproductive. I tried busying myself with gardening, but I didn't like it. I made household to-do lists, but I got through those chores in no time.

Gradually it dawned on me. *Maybe, just maybe, God has a plan for me. Maybe I should ask the Lord what he wants me to do. Maybe my "work" right now is to pray, starting at six o'clock every morning.* So that's what I did. I began to devote myself to prayer. As I did, I discovered a depth of relationship with Christ that would carry me to a place where I would finally understand my destiny for creating eternal wealth.

When you seek God's purpose through concerted prayer, he will communicate his will for your life. Knowing God's will creates joy in your heart and gives birth to a deep conviction. Once you know your purpose, you are empowered to develop strategies, set goals and objectives, embrace godly values, and establish relationships with others that will lead you down the pathway to creating eternal wealth. Because of your conviction, you will never be able to give up on your dream. But you'll never discover what that dream is without prayer.

Answering the Call

God is calling many people, especially women, to "Arise!" "Go!" and "Do!" The "arise" is a charge for them to elevate their thinking about the purpose for prosperity. The "go" is a call to action in the marketplace. And the "do" is a summons to engage in entrepreneurial pursuits for the purpose of creating and managing eternal wealth.

I believe this exciting journey cannot begin until a couple of things happen. First, people must conceive a great, God-inspired vision through intimacy with God birthed out of prayer. Next, they must learn how to fulfill their purpose by engaging in purposeful and profitable action.

When you think about God "calling" someone to action, I would wager a bet that you think he is calling that person into church ministry. For years people have assumed that if God calls you to do something, then it means he wants you to work in the church since the church is where God's business gets done. Pastors, teachers, evangelists, apostles, and prophets all receive calls from God to work in his church. God calls laypeople to work in his church as ushers, choir members, Sunday school teachers, and so on.

I have news for you. God does not confine the conduct of his business to work performed within the four walls of the church. In fact, he calls people to work for him in business, sports, media, arts and entertainment, law, politics, education, and health care. When you work in any one of these marketplace fields, you have a great opportunity to be a part of God's army of leaders devoted to creating a marketplace culture that conforms to his standards. God wants people with varying gifts and abilities, such as actors, lawyers, CEOs, senators, professional athletes, college deans, bankers, scientists, doctors, accountants, and other professionals to serve him in the marketplace.

When you answer God's call to marketplace ministry, a significant part of your ministry occurs in the marketplace. It means you understand the purpose for your prosperity. You understand the connections among the skills and abilities you possess, the work you do, the money you make, the people you influence, and your assignment in God's kingdom. That understanding strengthens your vision pillar, and you get that understanding from God. If you don't yet have that understanding, and so have not answered the call, God wants to give it to you. And don't be surprised if his process for getting it to you involves some pruning.

Conceiving the Vision

Albert Einstein once said, "We can't solve problems by using the same kind of thinking we used when we created them." Moving off the pathway to creating worldly wealth onto the pathway leading to the creation of eternal wealth requires an understanding of purpose, and when you understand purpose, you'll think at a higher level of awareness. Sometimes God will take you through a pruning process uniquely designed for you that will result in your discovering your purpose and elevating your thinking about your career and financial future.

God's role is to purge, wash, and speak purpose into our hearts. Our role is to submit to his process and embrace that purpose. When we cooperate with God's process and open our hearts to receive his purpose for our life, it begins the process that will eventually give birth to our vision for marketplace ministry.

Pruning is something we all must endure if we want to grow and be fruitful for God. Jesus said, "I am the true vine, and my Father is the gar-

---

Running with the Vision

Here are a few tips to help you conceive great, God-inspired vision for your life.

- Elevate your thinking. Have faith to call those "things that are not as though they were" (see Romans 4:17).
- If you think you don't have the ability to prosper, start telling yourself that you do, believe that you do, and then do something to build your confidence. Remember that the only place where success comes before work is in the dictionary.
- If you think that you're too old to produce anything significant at this stage of your life, remember Sarah (Abraham's wife). If you think you're too young, remember Mary the mother of Jesus. Believe in the vision and do what God tells you to do.
- If you are intimidated by people who don't think you know enough to do what God wants you to, remember the apostles.

dener. He cuts off every branch in me that bears no fruit, while every branch that does bear fruit he prunes so that it will be even more fruitful" (John 15:1-2). God's goal is maximum fruitfulness in our lives, so he lovingly and skillfully prunes away anything that interferes with his goal.

Leaving my job at AT&T was the beginning of God's pruning process in my life. Getting pruned was necessary for me, but it wasn't fun. I didn't eagerly pray, "Lord, cut me here. Please take away my passion for work and my ambition, goals, and plans." I winced and resisted with every snip of the shears. It was difficult to give up things that brought me comfort, satisfaction, and security and that added perceived value to my life. That's why

> They were not learned men, but because of their relationship with Christ, they changed the world.
> - If you're afraid to dream big dreams because you're afraid of success, remember that this is not about you anyway. It's about what God wants to do in and through you. Surrender to him!
> - If you're reluctant to take on new challenges because the idea of a new job, business, or career is overwhelming to you, remember that God is bigger than your fears or your problems. That means you are bigger than your fears or problems, because greater is he who is in you than he who is in the world (see 1 John 4:4 NKJV).
> - If you have failed at something in your past, use your failures as a foundation on which to build your future. Don't let past failures keep you from building future success.
> - If you don't have enough resources to fulfill the vision, take good care of the little you have. God will make it much.
>
> "Break up your unplowed ground; for it is time to seek the LORD until he comes and showers righteousness on you" (Hosea 10:12).

God had to do the pruning instead of me, because I would have gone too easy on myself. He knew just how much to cut away in order to maximize the new growth.

Pruning hurts because God often uses the stresses and disappointments of life to effect the change he wants in us. God uses difficult and unexpected life events to cause the change to happen. Pruning involves loss, but it is loss for the sake of gain. Just as the rosebush in the garden doesn't get to choose whether it will be pruned each season, so we don't get to choose our pruning seasons. It happens at God's appointed time, and it happens to clear our minds of selfish thoughts and cleanse us of behaviors and ways of thinking that would hinder further growth in our lives and keep us from discovering our purpose.

God does not act haphazardly; he does everything for a reason. He prunes our lifestyles, redirects our ambitions, and alters our paradigms so we can fulfill his plan and purpose for our lives. But we must let go of what God prunes from our lives in order to make room for what he wants to bloom in our lives. Pruning clears the way so new vision can blossom.

After I left AT&T Broadband, I enjoyed telling people that I had retired. No more traffic-congested commutes. No more sixty-hour workweeks, meetings, conference calls, endless e-mails to read, or calls to return. No more competing in the system, striving to stay ahead of the game, running fast, and working myself to a frazzle. No more corporate power struggles and being controlled by someone else's agenda. I had run out of gas and was taking a break. I was out of the rat race and considered myself a big winner.

It didn't take long to realize, however, that by following God's direction for my life, I had traded one kind of pain for another. God had removed me from the corporate world, kind of like a gardener digging up a plant, root-ball and all, and transplanted me to a place in his garden that was right for me but unfamiliar. I was still something of a wild plant, having pursued worldly wealth with abandon. The deadwood of my old, fruitless way of thinking about money and acquiring wealth had to be cut away so God could make me fruitful at creating eternal wealth. I had to change my thinking, change some relationships, embrace the change process, learn how to affirm who I was in Christ, and wait on God.

The process took some time and wasn't always fun. But through it all I discovered who I am in God's kingdom and his purpose for my life. I also conceived a God-inspired vision for my prosperity.

If I can make it through God's pruning and perfecting process, so can you. Here is what I learned about each step of the process that may be helpful to you on your journey to discovering your purpose. And remember, this entire process is wrapped in a cocoon of prayer.

1. Embracing purpose begins with a changed mind.

How often have you said to yourself, "I can't do it," "It won't work," "I tried that already," "I'm not good enough," "What will people think?" "I can't get the money," "No one will help me," and so on. God's purpose for your career may well challenge you to do something you've never done before. It can stretch your understanding of what you're capable of accomplishing, and so your immediate response to discovering his challenging new vision for your life might be self-doubt.

In my case the recurring unproductive thoughts were "Don't start a business," "You can't make it running a company," "Are you sure you have what it takes?" "Go back to working for someone else and forget your dreams." My negative thinking was even fueled by a friend who told me, "Julaine, you're the glue that holds an organization together, but you need someone to lead the organization." Unproductive thoughts of self-doubt had been a part of my life for years. But when I began to focus my attention on God and his Word, I also began to see myself fulfilling the purpose he had for me. It was then that I began to ignore those thoughts and what people said I couldn't do. My mind changed. The playwright George Bernard Shaw said it this way: "Progress is not possible without change; and those who cannot change their minds cannot change anything."

Since God's pruning process involves loss of some sort, it's not uncommon for people to start off by experiencing self-doubt. And if God uses job or economic loss of some sort to initiate your pruning process, that can easily trigger self-doubting thoughts. Have you ever lost a job you really loved or had a business deal go south? Have you ever lost large amounts of money in the stock market or suffered through bankruptcy? These events can cause even the most self-confident person to question his or her abilities.

You can, however, replace unproductive thinking with what God says. When you're going through pruning, daily inspirational reading from the Word of God, coupled with prayer and meditation, will change the condition of your heart and get rid of unproductive thinking. The secret is to remember that no matter how hard you try to stop thinking unproductive thoughts, they will continue to plague your mind until you fill your mind with the truth of God's Word and think on it.

The beauty of God's pruning process is that, as you increase the amount of time you spend with him and his Word, you will be motivated to learn more about God and his purpose for you in his kingdom. You'll also want to learn more about yourself, including your strengths, weaknesses, and potential. You will be motivated to understand how your unique gifts, skills, and abilities are linked to fulfillment of God's specific strategy for building his kingdom in the field he's calling you to. Over time you'll discover God's original intent for your life, and that discovery will empower you to pursue your purpose. So even if the price you have to pay is the loss of a great job or a source of financial security, the empowerment you gain from having a renewed mind and knowing your purpose is worth it.

Unproductive thinking tears you down. A mind renewed in God's Word builds you up.

2. *Prune away ineffective or unproductive relationships.*

When you're committed to cooperating with God's process of revealing purpose and conceiving great vision, be prepared to let go of ineffective or unproductive relationships. The old saying is true: "We become like the people we spend time with." Family and culture impact our ability to conceive great vision. Neighbors, friends, and business associates impact our ability to conceive great vision. Teachers and the media impact our ability to conceive great vision. And religious leaders who feed our spirits impact our ability to conceive great vision.

God's pruning process may require that we let go of people in our life who drain our energy, discourage us, lack faith, or otherwise sow complacency in our lives. Invite God to orchestrate the events that will result in the pruning of relationships that hinder your ability to understand your purpose and conceive the vision he has for you. Take a relationship inventory. Ask God to guide you as you assess whether you should let go of certain relationships. He will let you know which changes, if any, you should make in your relationships.

3. *Embrace change.*

Conceiving new vision and fulfilling our purpose requires that we embrace change, and generally speaking, people don't like change. Nevertheless, our ability to create eternal wealth hinges on our willingness to embrace new ideas and ways of thinking about our life and our money. We can abort our new vision and forfeit our purpose if we refuse to embrace change and to believe what God shows us about the purpose for our life, career, and prosperity.

What we believe about ourselves, our career, and our financial situation impacts our willingness to change. Our belief system acts as a type of filter.

Think of it like a pair of eyeglasses. If the lenses are dirty or the prescription is wrong, the glasses will hinder our ability to see clearly. So it is with our beliefs.

What we believe about ourselves and about what we can accomplish with our career or our money can actually hinder our willingness to work through the changes we need to make. Many times we limit what we do because of a lack of belief in ourselves or trust in God's power. When we change what we believe so that it aligns with God's Word, our vision becomes clearer. This is another reason why we must work hard at getting rid of unproductive thinking and unproductive relationships.

We are who God says we are! All the lies we've been told about ourselves, whether by society, family, our culture, or even our own thoughts, have to be washed away by the truth of God's Word. When we believe what God says about us and trust in his power, then the lens through which God's vision is cast will be clear. Our vision will not be distorted and we will embrace change in our lives.

4. *Begin to say what you see.*

Before we can begin to see the new vision materialize in our lives, we have to begin to say what we see. I'm talking about confessing with our lips the greatness of the Spirit in us and the greatness of what Christ wants to do in and through us before we see any evidence of its occurring.

It can be intimidating to speak out loud something that we can never pull off on our own. (In fact, if you're not intimidated by your new vision, then I suggest you keep seeking an understanding of the amazing things God wants to do through you, because more likely than not, his plans for your career and your money will be intimidating.) But saying what we "see" facilitates God's process of birthing great vision in our lives.

A pastor once told me that we believe 80 percent of what we confess and only 60 percent of what other people tell us. Changing what we say will change what we see in the natural. Daily self-affirmation strengthens our ability to believe the great vision God gives us.

Entrepreneurs, business leaders, and people who create wealth are the carriers of vision. It is important to watch carefully what we say to ourselves, our family, our coworkers, and our friends. What we say will either help or hurt our ability to give birth to our vision and create eternal wealth.

Sometimes people confuse affirmations with saying what you're not. Affirmation is not saying what you're not; it's saying what you are. For example, let's imagine that your vision is to lose some weight. A daily affirmation that says, "I'm not going to eat sugar and fat today," will only put sugar and fat on your mind and cause you to want to eat them all the more. But if you say, "I'm healthy and I make balanced choices about the foods I eat," you will find yourself doing just that.

When you begin to speak the new vision God has given you, make sure you affirm yourself and the vision by making it personal, positive, and in the present tense.

5. Wait on the Lord.

When we're in the midst of God's pruning process, our anxiety over our future can make us want to get on with life as soon as possible. Therefore, our first response to revealed purpose and new vision may be to quickly embrace new ideas and begin doing things to make it happen. But that's not how God works. If you can "make it happen" on your own, then it's probably not God's idea; it's your idea. Instead of rushing to create the end product of the vision (as was my usual response whenever I got a great idea), you need to learn to wait on God.

"Wait for what?" you might ask.

We need to wait for God to release us to do the work, and that won't happen until he knows we are prepared to do the work.

Developing the Heart to Carry the Vision

When God reveals the purpose that gives rise to new vision for our life, a period of preparation always precedes fulfillment of the purpose. The preparation period has several purposes. First, God uses it to clarify the vision. Second, he uses it to examine and test our level of courage and commitment to fulfilling the vision. Third, God sets about purging our hearts of any remaining obstacles that stand in the way of our achieving his purposes. Our character is continually refined through this waiting period and through God's clarification, examination, and purging process.

During the preparation period, your newly conceived vision for life will be clarified. Throughout this process, it's important to keep track of your experiences. God tells us through the prophet Habakkuk, "Write the vision and make it plain on tablets, that he may run who reads it" (Habak-kuk 2:2, NKJV). Clarifying our understanding of new vision begins by putting God's revealed purpose for us into words. I've already talked about the importance of speaking your new vision. In addition to saying what God shows you, write the vision. Keep it in front of your eyes. Share it with supportive friends. Writing the vision will help you understand the vision and will clear the way for planning your strategy and then doing it.

The process of writing the vision can take several months or even years. A helpful tool when you're in the process of writing the vision is a journal. Journaling your thoughts and experiences is a great daily exercise that will create a written record to help you remember what God speaks to you and what you discover about him, yourself, and your circumstances. I have been journaling for several years now. Whenever I get discouraged or confused about God's purposes for me, I go through my journal and reread some of the promises he has made to me. Then I can reconnect with the joy and excitement I've experienced along the way. Rereading journal entries helps me remember that I'm not standing still but making progress.

Before God sent the Israelites into the Promised Land, he sent in a small band of spies to check out the territory and sample some of its fruit (Numbers 13). The spies' job was to confirm the vision God had given them. But most of the spies were filled with doubt because of what they saw. They were overwhelmed by the obstacles since they focused on the giants in the land instead of the opportunities God had provided. Their focus revealed their lack of trust in him and unproductive thinking (they expected to fulfill the vision in their own strength using old tactics, and yet the giants looked far stronger). Only Joshua and Caleb believed that God would enable them to possess what he wanted them to have, no matter how overwhelming the obstacles seemed. And these two men of faith were the only ones among the spies who actually enjoyed God's promised provision.

When God shows us who we are in his kingdom and the greatness of the call he has in store for us, we too will go through a process of examination and testing. These are the steps God uses to make our election for the job sure.

Examining our resolve and testing our courage to fulfill God's vision involves wrestling with our old self, who wants to pursue old dreams in old ways. Fear and challenges arise when we can't see a connection between God's vision and satisfaction of our old desires. Fear and challenges also arise when we know we are ill equipped to accomplish the tasks associated with fulfilling the vision on our own. When these conditions converge, we'll struggle with whether our life will be defined by doing God's will or doing our will. It is at this point that we must decide whether we're willing to lay down our life, pick up our cross, and follow Jesus.

The only way to move to the place of total surrender to God's will is to allow him to purge our hearts of any remaining obstacles that stand in the way of our achieving his purposes. I found the purging part of the waiting process the most painful. Even after spending many years in God's pruning, purpose, and vision-producing process, I didn't want to let go of all aspects of my past, and I didn't want to totally do things his way because, frankly, I couldn't make a strong enough connection between doing things God's way where my career was concerned and achieving the desires of my heart.

I vividly recall the moment when God finally got through to me and I said an unconditional yes to his purpose for my life. It happened as I sat at the TV listening to a pastor tell her story about how she got started in ministry. This particular pastor's life got off to a rocky start. She was sexually abused as a child, her father committed suicide, and she was raised in poverty and surrounded by despair. When God saved her and called her into the ministry, she was so thrilled to do work for God that she was willing to do *anything* as long as it was in service to him. As she was recounting her early days in ministry, I was struck by the level of her devotion to God. She worked for a church at that time and her job basically consisted of janitorial work. She vacuumed the rugs and cleaned the toilets in the church. The attention she paid to detail was so pronounced that she even straightened the fringe on the edge of the carpet. Now she is co-pastor of a thriving church, has a worldwide TV ministry, and has helped millions of people.

I heard this story during the time in my own perfecting process when I was struggling to accept the fact that, in order to do what God wanted me to do, I would have to risk not ever working for someone in a corporate position again. It had been several years since I'd left AT&T. I had a pretty good understanding of what my purpose was; however, I wasn't sure how my fulfillment of that purpose was going to put me back in the race toward money, power, and prestige. I was also struggling with the transition from being an employee to being a business owner, primarily due to the uncertainty associated with not getting a biweekly paycheck. So every time I talked with God about my purpose, my side of the conversation went something like this: "Okay, God, I'll do the work you're calling me to do, but…" You can use your imagination to fill in the blank after the "but." The point is, "buts" always followed my statements of commitment to do the will of God. God wants our unconditional commitment and total surrender to do his will, not a partial surrender of will with self-absorbed conditions attached.

As I listened to this televangelist's testimony that day, tears began to stream down my face. My heart began to race as feelings of sorrow welled up in my soul. I knew I had fallen well short of the mark God was setting for me when he called me into marketplace ministry.

I sank to my knees and began to cry out to God for forgiveness. At that moment I saw a vision of a door closing behind me, the door that led to my past experiences as a corporate financial officer. I'm sure the evangelist had no idea that sharing her testimony would affect me the way it did. I know she has shared it on many occasions. But on this day that testimony sparked a spiritual reaction in my soul that pushed me from partial to total commitment to do the will of God, no matter what the cost.

Something had changed inside, and I knew I would never return to my past; it was over. I would not be returning to the career of chief financial officer that I had once so enjoyed. For the first time I was able to say, "God, I will do whatever you want me to do," and there was no "but" at the end of the sentence or in my heart. I had no idea how following Jesus was going to impact me financially, but I didn't care about that. All I wanted was to do his will.

Discovering our purpose and developing new vision requires us to devote ourselves to periods of learning and to be willing to examine our dreams and desires in the light of God's Word and his Spirit. If you can't stand spending time alone with God, you will have difficulty developing your divine vision and discovering your purpose, because this is a process that takes place with him alone. If you don't know how or have time to pray, the process will be aborted. You can receive encouragement from others, but you can't walk through the process of discovering your purpose and conceiving vision with a crowd. It's you and God, so make time for yourself with him and learn how to pray. God rewards those who diligently seek him. He will show you who you are and what he has for you to do, so keep asking, keep knocking, and keep seeking God.

Are you ready to begin praying for God's will for your career and finances? Perhaps the following prayer would be a good place to start: "Lord, place inside my heart your vision for my future, place inside my heart the details of your plan, place inside my heart the strategies that fulfill your purpose, for I desire to do your will. Amen."

The seven stewardship principles and the principles for building relationships with our family and others, introduced in part 1, represent the rules of God's house pertaining to stewardship of his resources. For people who desire to maintain an intimate relationship with God while fulfilling their God-given purpose for prosperity, applying his principles is not an option; it is a requirement. All of God's principles, those for stewardship and those pertaining to other areas of our life, are essential for our personal development and prosperity in his kingdom. Obeying God's Word and following his principles is key to being able to do his will, produce and manage wealth, and live a prosperous life while also escaping the corruption of the world. That's because doing things God's way causes our souls to prosper.

In the next chapter we'll look at how spiritual assets work in us to develop our soul's prosperity and increase our workplace effectiveness.

QUESTIONS FOR REFLECTION AND DISCUSSION

1. What is your vision for creating eternal wealth?

2. Are you ready and willing to do whatever God asks you, even if it means giving up financial or material possessions, to pursue your purpose?

3. List the things you need to let go of or to start doing more of in order to fulfill your purpose. Commit these things to God in daily prayer.

> Efforts to create eternal wealth succeed only when you add something to faith.

Chapter 8

THE ESSENTIALS OF SOUL PROSPERITY

Federal prosecutors in Chicago have charged twenty-two store owners and employees with stealing at least $16 million from the state's food stamp program. "The electronic food stamp program—called Link—was launched in Illinois in 1997 to combat rampant fraud in the paper food-stamp program....But cheaters quickly found ways to steal from the new, electronic food-stamp system too." For example, a welfare recipient might take to a grocery store a Link credit card credited for $100. "The store clerk swipes the card through a government computer and takes credit for $100 in phony food sales. Then, the clerk hands $70 to the welfare recipient, keeping the rest as profit." No product actually exchanges hands.[1]

Fraud in Medicare and Medicaid are believed to account for around $33 billion nationally each year. There are many kinds of scams. For example, a former nightclub owner made millions after he obtained a Medicare license without a background check and then opened a home health agency through which he charged Medicare $86 for each home visit instead of the actual sum of $16 to $22 he paid a nurse. Another scam artist accumulated $7 million over time by charging $5 and $7 for gauze surgical dressings that were worth only a penny apiece.[2]

Robert, a partner in the accounting firm Arthur Anderson's business consulting unit, asked one of the firm's young managers for an estimate to produce a CD-ROM for a large European bank. The CD-ROM was part of a proposal to help the bank coordinate its compliance manuals and ethics policies and design a brief program to introduce them to employees in the wake of a merger. The manager came back with an estimate of $50,000. "That's as high as I can legitimately go," he told the partner. "That's the price for my top of the line."

Robert stared at him, disgusted. "We don't do anything for $50,000."

The manager slunk out of the partner's office in the full knowledge that when he returned he had better have generously padded the price.

Soon the head of the firm's ethics and responsible business practices group got the same kind of dressing-down for the estimate she supplied for her part of the proposal. She wrote of the encounter,

> "What's this $75,000?" he shouted.... This is the big time, young lady." (I didn't take that as a compliment.) "What kind of a consultant are you?"
>
> "A good one....And for our piece of the project, that's a high-end estimate."

But Robert was having none of it. "You make that $150,000," he ordered. "Back into it."

In the end, the estimate for the entire proposal was $600,000.[3]

You probably can't imagine yourself ever *thinking* about perpetrating, let alone actually *perpetrating*, the kinds of fraud described in these stories just so you could make a buck. But unfortunately, these types of fraud, embezzlement, and corporate corruption are commonplace in our marketplace today. They serve as a strong indicator that too many people believe the end somehow justifies the means when it comes to creating wealth.

A desire for money and success can lead people to foolishly believe they can take care of their career and finances their way even if their strategy conflicts with God's principles. Misdirected ambition and unchecked greed produce destructive behaviors. And these culprits of destructive behaviors don't discriminate. The rich and powerful, the poor and disenfranchised, and even Christians are susceptible to the lure of greed and misdirected ambition.

But behaviors don't have to result in criminal convictions in order to violate God's rules. Success earned by honest, law-abiding means can be intoxicating and can cause Christians to lose sight of the fact that obeying God is a higher priority than achieving financial success. When we are blinded by money and success, we can't see God, and when we can't see God, we are apt to disobey him.

Engaging in purposeful and profitable action for creating eternal wealth takes place in the marketplace. And working in the marketplace exposes us to all types of people, principles, and practices, many of which are grounded in ideals that are worldly and evil. That is why, before God called us to work for him in the marketplace, he prepared a way for us to avoid the trap of corruption by giving us access to everything we need to live a life pleasing to him. That life starts when we put our faith in Christ, and it is strengthened as we grow in our knowledge of who Christ is. By putting our faith in Christ and getting to know him, we position ourselves to receive God's promises, including his promise to give us the power to create wealth.

Getting to know Christ happens as we study God's Word and begin to understand his commands and principles. When we keep our focus on fulfilling God's purposes, obeying him becomes paramount to everything we do. Obeying God builds character. And building our character in the image of Christ is God's plan for the prosperity of our souls—the prosperity that enables us to work in the marketplace, make and manage financial resources, escape worldly corruption, and create eternal wealth.

Soul Prosperity

Soul prosperity is a key component for creating the kind of wealth that abundantly provides for your needs in this life *and* stores up great treasure in heaven. Your soul is comprised of your mind (thinking), will (choosing), and emotions (feeling). Prosperity means making your way a success. Soul prosperity, then, means making the way of your thinking a success, making the way of your choosing a success, and making the way of your feeling a success.

Soul prosperity is the result of an ongoing, self-reflective process aimed at the development of character. The desired outcome of this self-reflective process is the development of a mind, will, and emotions that are conformed to the image of Christ. According to God's agenda and the principles of his economy, we are to seek first his kingdom and his righteousness, and all things will be given to us as well (Matthew 6:33). Thus soul prosperity happens when we devote ourselves to seeking life in God's kingdom above all things—and that means seeking to obey him, thereby developing character based on his principles or standards. Scripture teaches that the kingdom of God is not a matter of boastful talk or material things, but it is righteousness, peace, joy, and power in the Holy Spirit (see Romans 14:17 and 1 Corinthians 4:20). Soul prosperity, then, develops when we seek first to think and behave in a manner exemplifying the standards of righteousness, peace, joy, and power in the Holy Spirit.

Building on the Foundation

Wouldn't it be great if all it took to create eternal wealth was to develop character exemplifying the spiritual attributes of righteousness, peace, joy, and power in the Holy Spirit? Think about it. You walk into the church one Sunday, spiritually and financially impoverished. But after listening to a soul-saving message, you make the right decision and give your life to Christ. You respond to the altar call, pray the sinner's prayer, are water-baptized, and receive the baptism of the Holy Spirit. You leave the church service a new person, full of the Holy Spirit and power, rich in God's Spirit and ready to claim all his promises, including the promise to give you the power to create wealth.

As Monday morning dawns, your bank balance is still lower than you want, but you have faith that God is going to help you prosper spiritually and financially. Your spirit and optimism are high. There's only one problem: you don't know how to acquire greater amounts of money. You return to the church service week after week, year after year, and continue to be fed spiritual milk and meat. Your soul is beginning to prosper as you learn more about God's Word and begin to practice your faith. You're growing spiritually, spending quality time with God in prayer, and beginning to understand your God-given purpose. You tithe faithfully and give offerings whenever you can. However, you didn't come from a family with money; your parents were barely able to make ends meet. The jobs you've had in the past, and the one you have today, have barely provided for your needs.

You don't have a mentor or coach to help you develop your effectiveness in the marketplace. Entrepreneurs don't run in your family, and the only wealthy people you know are the ones on TV. You know God desires for you to prosper, and in fact you believe you're on the road to soul prosperity. But you also know that your faith and obedience somehow fall short of fully equipping you with what you need to create financial wealth, because no matter how hard you believe, your bank account balance just won't increase.

Or perhaps having enough money has never been an issue for you. You walk into the church one Sunday morning spiritually impoverished and financially rich. You're financially successful and proud of your accomplishments. You're also stressed out and your life lacks peace and joy. You make the decision to give your life to Christ. You respond to the altar call, pray the sinner's prayer, are water-baptized, and receive the baptism of the Holy Spirit. You leave the church service a new person, full of the Holy Spirit and power, and ready to claim all of God's promises, including the promise to live the abundant life. But your career demands keep you from spending time in prayer like you want to. You pay your tithes but find yourself neglecting the work God wants you to do, such as spending more time with your family or helping out at the church, because making money is central to your life. Although you want to live a more balanced lifestyle, there's no way to maintain your career and financial success unless you keep up the pace you've set at work. You've achieved what was most important to you—career and financial success—without Christ, so you don't see what your relationship with God has to do with how you make your money. That part of your life is under *your* control. Sure, the stress is there and you've made mistakes along the way. But all in all, you consider yourself successful. In addition to your wealth, all you need are greater levels of joy, peace, and fulfillment in your life. You want that abundant life that you've learned about and that you know Christ wants you to have.

It's frustrating when you have a dream and don't know how to make that dream a reality. Someone once said success is your dream with work clothes on. Knowing about God's promise to give us the power to create wealth and to live an abundant life (the precepts of eternal wealth) but not knowing how to put on your work clothes to make God's promise your reality is frustrating.

There is indeed more to creating eternal wealth than having faith in God. It begins there. However, as we proactively develop our character, our efforts toward changing our way of thinking about money, success, and our financial situation will succeed only if we add some things to our faith. To create wealth, we need to add to our faith such things as self-discipline, know-how, leadership skills, and hard work. To live a life full of joy that emanates from the fulfillment of our God-given purpose, we must understand that in God's kingdom wealth does not equate to money. You can be full of faith and financially poor. Or you can be financially rich and spiritually poor. God has given us the means to correct both of these situations. Let's start by taking a look at his direction for changing our financial situation when we have faith but lack finances.

Second Peter 1:5-8 provides some valuable insight into the soul-prospering attributes we must possess in addition to faith to develop wealth-producing capabilities.

> Make every effort to add to your faith goodness; and to goodness, knowledge; and to knowledge, self-control; and to self-control, perseverance; and to perseverance, godliness; and to godliness, brotherly kindness; and to brotherly kindness, love. For if you possess these qualities in increasing measure, they will keep you from being ineffective and unproductive in your knowledge of our Lord Jesus Christ.

God's advice for how to live an effective and productive life in Christ, and hence for how to maximize soul prosperity, is to "make every effort to *add* to your faith..." (emphasis added). As our souls prosper, we are able to prosper in every area of our life, including the work we do (3 John 2 NKJV). Faith in Jesus Christ is the doorway to God's forgiveness and acceptance, and we don't have to add anything to faith to receive salvation. But we're not in heaven yet; God saved us and left us on earth to work for him. More is necessary for doing work that creates financial wealth than saving faith because to create financial wealth you must know how to make and effectively manage financial and human resources. This is one reason why Peter gave us a list of soul-enriching qualities to "possess... in increasing measure": goodness, knowledge, self-control, perseverance, godliness, brotherly kindness, and love. These qualities, added to our faith, produce wisdom for doing work that creates wealth.

As you can easily see in the brief definitions below, each quality, which I collectively refer to as *spiritual capital,* is a great asset for daily living, success in the workplace and leadership development.

Goodness: moral excellence demonstrated by virtuous thoughts, feelings, and actions.

A person who is good, honest, truthful, and just in his or her professional and financial dealings will experience greater success in the long run than someone who is underhanded and dishonest with money. The Golden Rule tells us we should do unto others as we would have them do unto us. When we demonstrate goodness, we treat others with respect, dignity, and equality and are sensitive to their needs and emotions. Most people don't want to be lied to, deceived by partial information, offended, or injured by another person's selfish focus or thoughtless, rude, or insensitive behavior. People don't want to be defrauded out of their money or property or be discriminated against. When we follow the Golden Rule and do work with goodness, we avoid these negative behaviors and we have a positive influence on others. And when we add goodness to our faith, we are also quick to seek and give forgiveness if we ever do something to offend others or when we are wronged by them. Goodness produces wisdom for wealth in relationships. It protects us from the corruption of the world that causes people pursuing worldly wealth to lie, backstab, sabotage, and betray others on their way to the top of the corporate ladder.

Knowledge: wisdom and understanding demonstrated by competency and awareness.

We need more than spiritual and biblical knowledge to produce financial wealth. To be productive in the marketplace, we also need wisdom and understanding about the world's system. Education and work experience increase wisdom and understanding, enhance our awareness, and develop our character as a leader. Our work experience and business relationships help to mold our understanding of how the marketplace works and expand our knowledge base, expertise, proficiency, and skill levels. They improve our competency and awareness of how things work in the real world. In addition to work experience, we also need knowledge that comes from education and training. Education and training in the areas of leadership, organizational behavior, interpersonal skills, and team building help us understand how to manage human resources. Education and training in the fields of technology, marketing, sales, finance, law, and business administration prepare us to own and/or manage business operations. Education and training in a particular trade or craft help us master our gift. In general, we need know-how derived from education and work experience to develop our gifts and perfect our skills and abilities. Knowledge protects us from ignorance. It helps us know ourselves, develop our capabilities, and understand how to get things done in the workplace. Knowledge produces wisdom for wealth in know-how. Knowledge empowers us so we can compete in the marketplace and create wealth just as successfully as someone who doesn't have faith in Christ.

Self-control: mastering desires and passions, especially sensual appetites.

"Self-control means control over one's own emotions, actions, desires, and passions."[4] We need the inner discipline to say a decisive yes to the right uses of our time and resources and a firm no to the wrong uses. Working to produce wealth takes hard work and requires a lot of energy. When we are self-controlled, we have a clear vision and are focused on achieving our wealth-producing goals. We concentrate on developing success-oriented, career-enhancing behaviors. We maintain healthy eating and drinking habits and get appropriate rest and exercise to increase our energy and stamina to do the work. We manage our time so as not to neglect daily prayer and reading and meditating on God's Word. We take the initiative to educate ourselves and increase our mental agility. We take care of ourselves physically, mentally, and spiritually. Building wealth requires us to make financial investments and work in a marketplace that is subject to unexpected change and events. But when we are self-controlled, we adapt to changing circumstances and bad news without being easily frightened or angered. We don't lose control. And our mastery over our sensual appetites helps us to avoid inappropriate behaviors such as overindulging in alcohol, using illegal drugs or abusing prescription drugs, committing sexual indiscretions, entering into excessive debt, gambling, and the like—behaviors that can detract from our efforts to produce eternal wealth. Prime Minister Margaret Thatcher said that disciplining yourself to do what you know is important and right, although difficult, is the high road to pride (self-confidence), self-esteem, and personal satisfaction. Self-control produces wisdom for wealth in self-discipline. Exercising self-control protects us from the corruption of the world caused by acting on desires to do whatever we want, when we want, and in the way we want in order to maximize our bottom line or satisfy sensual appetites and self-centered interest.

Perseverance: steadfast endurance in purpose and loyalty even in the heat of great trial and suffering.

Perseverance stems from self-control. It's what makes us persist and remain constant, doing the right thing and even the hard thing in order to achieve our goal in the face of obstacles. Perseverance is the foundation of sustained success and long-term personal achievement. Some people give up too easily. They'll set their mind on accomplishing a goal, but as soon as adversity comes, they'll give up instead of plowing through. Some people get close to success but then give up just before their breakthrough. When we are working to build wealth for the benefit of God's enterprise, we will meet resistance. Anytime we set our hearts and minds on doing something for God, resistance will come. We must be steadfast and faithful even in the heat of great trial if we want to fulfill the plans he has for our prosperity. We have to stand under the pressure of work-related stress, competing priorities, distractions, and unreasonable demands or expectations that can try to keep us from reaching our goal. Creating eternal wealth is a long-term process. It requires focus and commitment. You may take a lot of flak for managing your work life and finances God's way. You may be tempted to embrace the world's self-centered economic system when it appears that track to riches will help you enjoy more money and things sooner than going God's way. But perseverance stays the course, refuses to compromise righteousness for ungodly gain, and allows God's economic principles to bear lasting fruit. Perseverance produces wisdom for wealth in faithfulness.

Godliness: deep reverence and respect for God and devotion to his ways.
Constantly submitting our will regarding our career and finances to God's will helps to keep his purposes clearly in view and demonstrates our devotion to him. Demonstrating godly characteristics such as competence, determination, decisiveness, optimism, strength, courage, and commitment to excellence produces good work. These characteristics help us stand up for our convictions and values even if it means risking criticism or persecution. They help us risk loss for the sake of doing what we believe is right. Our outlook stays hopeful when we demonstrate godliness, because we expect the best outcome. We can accept the reality of a situation but know that with hard work, focus, resilience, and God's favor, a positive outcome is possible. When we commit ourselves to godliness, it creates a significant connection between us and God. And that connection encourages and inspires us. The good work we produce as a result of demonstrating the characteristics of godliness pays dividends in the marketplace in the form of increased responsibilities, sphere of influence, and income. Godliness protects us from the corruption of the world that causes people to participate in and/or promote morally decaying and character destroying business activities for the sake of creating wealth. Godliness produces wisdom for wealth in righteousness.

Brotherly kindness: treating people as if they are family—in the most positive sense.
We want the best for our loved ones in every way. That should be our attitude toward everyone we deal with, including people we work with in the marketplace. Demonstrating kindness toward those we work with contributes to the development of our leadership skills. People who demonstrate kindness lead with compassion, empathy, sympathy, and nurturing qualities that give them a distinct advantage when it comes to influencing

and inspiring others. In the book *Why the Best Man for the Job Is a Woman*, the author points out that in our high tech era, when more and more people "conduct business through e-mail, voice mail, passwords, and PINs, leaders who succeed today—and will continue to do so in the future—are those who guide with a strong, personal 'bedside manner.'"[5] These "new paradigm leaders" are "interested in people, and listen and communicate in ways that build rapport and level the learning field, rather than distancing themselves from colleagues."[6] Leading with kindness engenders loyalty and respect. It also protects us from the corruption of the world that causes people pursuing career success and wealth to perpetrate offenses against others and atrocities on the environment for the sake of making money. Kindness produces wisdom for wealth in leadership.

Love: self-sacrifice that always puts others first.

This is *agape*, the supreme expression of love in the Bible and the motivating factor in God's economy. Christ laid down his life in love for us; we are to lay down our lives to serve him and others with our gifts, skills, and abilities. Jesus said that if we want to be great among people, then we must become a servant to others (Matthew 20:26). We must be willing to offer (serve) our gifts, skills, and abilities to others to help them develop as a person and/or fulfill their purpose. Service in this regard does not preempt compensation; you can be a servant volunteer or you can be a servant and receive compensation. Of course, in the context of creating wealth, we are talking about serving our gifts in the marketplace for compensation, either in the form of wages or profits. And our service should be done out of love and an attitude of caring. Love produces servant leaders who are interested and concerned about the development of others. When love is the motivation behind our leadership, we develop strong, healthy, and respect-based relationships. People feel appreciated, validated, and accepted when we lead with love, and that increases our ability to influence and inspire others to do great work. When we serve our gifts to the world with love and care, it produces great personal satisfaction as well as financial wealth. Love produces wisdom for wealth in service to others.

The apostle Peter knew the key to wisdom for eternal wealth. He knew the essentials for a prosperous soul. That shouldn't be a surprise since he personally spent time with Jesus, the Author of abundant living. What I find so marvelous about 2 Peter 1:5-8 is that when you do what these verses tell you and position yourself to create wealth God's way, you don't have to fear failure or loss. When failure comes, you'll know how to pick yourself up and start again. When economic loss happens, you'll dust off your work clothes and get back to work. If you lose money, you'll work hard to make some more.

Spiritual Capital

1. *Goodness:* moral excellence demonstrated by virtuous thoughts, feelings, and actions
2. *Knowledge:* wisdom and understanding demonstrated by competency and awareness
3. *Self-control:* mastering desires and passions, especially sensual appetites
4. *Perseverance:* steadfast endurance in purpose and loyalty even in the heat of great trial and suffering
5. *Godliness:* deep reverence and respect for God and devotion to his ways
6. *Brotherly kindness:* treating people as if they are family—in the most positive sense
7. *Love:* self-sacrifice that always puts others first

Adding spiritual capital to your faith is an ongoing effort. It's work. But so is changing your financial situation or creating wealth. When you add spiritual capital to your faith in increasing measure, the wisdom for wealth that you produce will be well worth the effort. That's why King Solomon, the richest king who ever lived, wrote in Proverbs 4:7, "Wisdom is the principal thing; therefore, get wisdom. And in all your getting, get understanding" (NKJV).

God did not leave you alone to face your wealth-related challenges. And if you created wealth before you gave your life to Christ and therefore have been operating under the false assumption that God doesn't need to be involved in your business dealings, it's only because you don't yet understand that in his kingdom wealth and money aren't the same thing. Remember that your ability to create wealth in God's kingdom was and will always be a function of the synergy that is created as you partner with his Spirit by adding spiritual capital to your faith and the Spirit's influence to your work life. You're not running this race alone!

Spiritual Power for a Prosperous Soul

Soul prosperity is anchored in the understanding that, ultimately, God is the source of any and all wealth we enjoy. He has been teaching his people this truth since Old Testament times.

When God through Moses delivered the Israelites from Egypt, his plan was to march them right into Canaan—the Promised Land, which he had promised to Abraham and his descendants generations earlier. Sadly, a journey that should have taken only a few weeks stretched into forty years because the people refused to believe God's promise that they could occupy the land.

Once the disbelieving generation had died off, God once again led Israel to the border of the Promised Land. Before entering, Moses reminded them of the importance of following God's law. The book of Deuteronomy is that reminder. One particular lesson the people needed related to wealth, because their standard of living was about to change dramatically. The Israelites had been wandering nomads in the wilderness for forty years and slaves in Egypt for four hundred years before that. Life for generations had been essentially hand to mouth, but soon they would take up residence in the land of milk and honey. God intended to get the people spiritually ready to transition from slave laborers to prosperous landowners.

> When you have eaten and are satisfied, praise the LORD your God for the good land he has given you. Be careful that you do not forget the LORD your God, failing to observe his commands, his laws and his decrees that I am giving you this day. Otherwise, when you eat and are satisfied, when you build fine houses and settle down, and when your herds and flocks grow large and your silver and gold increase and all you have is multiplied, then your heart will become proud and you will forget the LORD your God, who brought you out of Egypt, out of the land of slavery.... You may say to yourself, "My power and the strength of my hands have produced this wealth for me." But remember the LORD your God, for it is he who gives you the ability to produce wealth, and so confirms his covenant, which he swore to your forefathers, as it is today.
>
> If you ever forget the LORD your God and follow other gods and worship and bow down to them, I testify against you today that you will surely be destroyed. Like the nations the LORD destroyed before you, so you will be destroyed for not obeying the LORD your God. (Deuteronomy 8:10-14, 17-20)

The Hebrew word translated "wealth" in verse 18 of this passage is *chayil*, meaning "a force or power that results in a state of abundance."

Many Christians today simply equate *chayil* with money, and they use this verse to insist that God has equipped his people to make lots of money. To be sure, money is intrinsic to the meaning of *chayil*. But the word means much more than just money and the things it can buy.

Chayil—the power or force that results in a state of abundance—is the wisdom and character that enable you to possess, control, and multiply material possessions. Maintaining a focus on creating *chayil* keeps our center of attention on God because he is our source of wisdom, and Christ is the example of character we want to emulate in creating *chayil*.

If you equate money with *chayil*, you will think money is the power or force that results in your state of abundance. In your quest to create wealth, you will seek money and exalt it as the source of your ability to possess, control, and multiply material possessions and to live an abundant life, instead of seeking God. If you fail to keep your center of attention on God, and instead view money as your source of wealth, Moses said, "Your heart will become proud and you will forget the Lord your God" and "you will surely be destroyed." In other words, creating wealth without seeking God first won't profit you at all in the long run, either physically or spiritually.

Robert Kiyosaki, author of *Rich Dad's Cashflow Quadrant*, defines wealth as "the number of days you can survive, without physically working (or anyone else in your household physically working) and still maintain your standard of living."[7] I like this definition because, like *chayil*, it broadens the meaning of wealth beyond mere money. Building and controlling wealth has to do with having wisdom and character to properly think about, respond to, and manage your economic and personal life situations.

Chayil is created by faithful people who possess increasing levels of spiritual capital and who develop the wisdom and character needed to pursue their God-given purpose and to rightly create and manage material and human resources. It is only by fulfilling our God-given purpose and creating *chayil* that we are able to experience abundant living. The power that God gives us to create *chayil* is the power of the Holy Spirit. The Holy Spirit works in and through us, increasing our wisdom and helping us develop the character we need to fulfill our God-given purpose and to deeply understand and create *chayil*—a financial force with a divine source.

The power of the Holy Spirit is unleashed through faith and such selfless soul qualities as goodness, knowledge, self-control, perseverance, godliness, kindness, and love. The power of the Holy Spirit for creating eternal wealth stands in stark contrast to how the world views power for creating wealth. Whereas God's power is something to be received by faith, the world's power is seen as something to be grasped by whatever means possible. The world's power is self-directed for personal profit. Power-grabbing, wealth-creating, and even fraudulent moneymaking tactics are often rationalized in terms of self-preservation or worldly philosophical and economic wisdom. Those who are intoxicated by the world's power measure success by how much money they control. Hence we have accounts of unbridled ambition leading to broken relationships, immoral business practices, fraud, embezzlement, and theft in the marketplace today.

> **A Financial Force with a Divine Source**
>
> *Chayil* (Heb.): a force or power that results in a state of abundance

When the power of God's Spirit works through us to accomplish his purposes, we don't need to follow the selfish, corrupt tactics of the world (which are really expressions of the sinful nature) to create wealth. We allow the Holy Spirit to work through us, from the inside out, to impact the world and generate *chayil* for his kingdom.

As we're filled with faith, increasing amounts of spiritual capital, and the Holy Spirit, we produce *chayil* and we advance God's enterprises in our families and in the world. A number of other good qualities of a prosperous soul come into play.

1. *Increased self-confidence.*

We are more assured because of God's protection and power. When we are operating in his power and for his purposes, there is no obstacle we cannot overcome. "The salvation of the righteous comes from the LORD; he is their stronghold in time of trouble. The LORD helps them and delivers them; he delivers them from the wicked and saves them, because they take refuge in him" (Psalm 37:39-40).

2. *Willingness to take risks.*

We are willing to step out in faith at God's command, even when it seems foolish. When the nation of Israel was ready to cross the Jordan River and occupy the Promised Land, Joshua commanded the priests carrying the ark to stand in the river. It must have seemed crazy to some people, because there was no way they could cross the mighty Jordan by walking. But the priests obeyed, and God caused the river to be "cut off and stand up in a heap" (Joshua 3:13). The entire nation walked across on a dry riverbed. A prosperous soul that is willing to take risks, including financial risks, in obedience to God will experience miraculous results.

3. *Greater level of trust.*

We believe in God and his process. Job lost virtually everything he owned. But even in the darkest and most painful moment of his life, Job was able to say about God, "Though he slay me, yet will I hope in him" (Job 13:15). A prosperous soul's trust in God does not rise and fall with circumstances. We are focused on doing God's will no matter what the cost. We say in the midst of our difficulties and challenges as Jesus said in the garden, "Not as I will, but as you will" (Matthew 26:39).

4. Optimistic attitude.

We enjoy a positive and hopeful outlook. The psalmist wrote, "I lift up my eyes to the hills—where does my help come from? My help comes from the LORD, the Maker of heaven and earth" (Psalm 121:1-2). As long as God lives and rules, we his children are never without hope. No matter how dark it gets, when we look up, our help is there.

5. Success orientation.

We are focused on accomplishments instead of defeats. "Let us fix our eyes on Jesus, the author and perfecter of our faith, who for the joy set before him endured the cross, scorning its shame, and sat down at the right hand of the throne of God. Consider him who endured such opposition from sinful men, so that you will not grow weary and lose heart" (Hebrews 12:2-3). Jesus looked past the seeming defeat of the cross, overjoyed at the victory of redemption he saw on the horizon. He calls us and empowers us to follow his example by fulfilling our God-given purpose no matter what the cost.

6. Greater levels of strength and courage:

We will not fear bad news. Some people live in dread of waking up some morning to news of recession, depression, or other financial crisis. But "a righteous man…will have no fear of bad news; his heart is steadfast, trusting in the LORD" (Psalm 112:6-7). The power behind our ability to create wealth is not the world's financial system. It's in the Lord, and he is impervious to failure or loss of any kind. He empowers us to face difficult obstacles and unseen foes. Joshua challenged God's people, "Be strong and courageous. Do not be terrified; do not be discouraged, for the LORD your God will be with you wherever you go" (Joshua 1:9). We face all economic challenges and approach all our financial decisions and transactions knowing that God is right there with us, giving us wisdom.

7. Increased social consciousness.

We feel and express compassion for people in need and we act as peacemakers in times of conflict. Jesus felt compassion for hurting people and acted on his compassion to meet needs. Walking in his power, we can do the same, just as the Good Samaritan ministered compassionately by sharing his time, energy, and resources. Financial friction tends to bring out the worst in people. They get territorial and defensive, ready to fight for what's theirs. Since we love God more than his material gifts, we can be instruments of peace in times of conflict over money. As Jesus said, "Blessed are the peacemakers, for they will be called sons of God" (Matthew 5:9).

Adding spiritual capital to our faith in increasing measure and relying on the power of God's Holy Spirit to produce *chayil* (wealth-creating character and wisdom) are steps that produce leaders in the marketplace with a heart for God and prosperous souls. Imagine for a moment what types of leaders were the persons involved in the stories about the welfare, Medicare, and corporate fraud I shared at the beginning of this chapter. Obviously, they didn't have a heart for God or an understanding of their God-given purpose. I doubt their souls were prosperous. When you think about the people you consider to be good leaders or bad leaders, the patterns you notice in their behaviors shape your opinion. Good leaders are usually described as visionary, competent, trustworthy, positive, dependable, caring, and good at communicating, whereas bad leaders are described as inconsistent, incompetent, pessimistic, not caring about anyone else, and unwilling to share information. A person's reputation as a leader, good or bad, is a reflection of his or her character. I find it interesting to note that the common behaviors of good leaders reflect purpose-driven persons who possess the attributes of courage, caring, self-control, optimism, and love—attributes of the Holy Spirit and the same attributes found in spiritual capital. These attributes of a great and Spirit-led leader become part of those who focus on developing the prosperity of their soul and fulfilling their God-given assignment.

To follow God's will for your life and to develop a prosperous soul, you must be driven by faith and a desire to obey him. Adding spiritual capital to faith and being filled with the Holy Spirit makes you productive and effective in the knowledge that it is God who gives you the power to create *chayil* wealth—a financial force with a divine source. It is also the secret to developing you into a marketplace leader who knows how to fulfill your purpose and, in the process, create eternal wealth.

The world's financial system, especially America's economy, provides a great marketplace in which to pursue our purpose and put our wealth-creating skills to the test. We know the system isn't perfect; it has flaws. But for those of us who are empowered by God's vision and a prosperous soul, the world's financial system offers a marvelous opportunity to make and manage money for the purpose of creating eternal wealth.

But the challenge is not for the faint of heart nor the foolish. We need to understand the risks as well as the rewards of capitalism before we embark upon any wealth-creating strategy. This is the place where work and determination come into play.

In the last few chapters of the book, we'll take a close look at the aspects of purposeful and profitable action that result in entrepreneurial efforts, strategic management of finances, and relationship building. But before we do, in the next chapter we're going to take an honest look at the state of the world's financial system, including some of its problems—problems we are going to have to face.

Questions for Reflection and Discussion

1. Which type(s) of spiritual capital do you need to add to your faith to increase your wisdom for wealth and soul prosperity?

2. In what ways does your leadership and workplace behavior already reflect attributes associated with spiritual capital?

3. Do you view money or God's power as your source of wealth, and why?

4. In what ways do you need to change your approach to making money so that you can create *chayil*?

" The problems associated with America's

economic system generate

opportunities for creating eternal wealth. "

Chapter 9

THE AMERICAN DREAM REVISITED

Negro spirituals are eloquent expressions of the aspirations of African American slaves. The following lyrics speak of the hope that slaves had for a time when they would experience the prosperity of God's kingdom.

> I got a robe, you got a robe
> All o' God's chillun got a robe
> When I get to heab'n I'm goin' to put on my robe
> I'm goin' to shout all ovah God's Heab'n
>
> Heab'n, Heab'n
> Ev'rybody talkin' 'bout heab'n ain't goin' dere
> Heab'n, Heab'n
> I'm goin' to shout all ovah God's Heab'n
>
> I got shoes, you got shoes
> All o' God's chillun got shoes

When I get to heab'n I'm goin' to put on my shoes
I'm goin' to walk all ovah God's Heab'n

Heab'n, Heab'n
Ev'rybody talkin' 'bout heab'n ain't goin' dere
Heab'n, Heab'n
I'm goin' to walk all ovah God's Heab'n[1]

The poverty and brutality that marked the slaves' lives stood in stark contrast to the promise for deliverance and peace in Christ Jesus. Their only hope was that one day they would go to heaven, where they would finally experience the joy of life in God's kingdom. In heaven they would find wealth, riches, and peace. In heaven they would be adorned with beautiful clothes and have shoes to wear. In heaven all their material needs would be met.

But the slaves also knew that some of the people who were talking about heaven were not going to get to live there. For the slaves experienced firsthand the contradiction between the way they were treated by their slave owners, who taught them about Christianity, and the love that God has commanded all his people to demonstrate to one another. Songs like this one, then, not only helped slaves endure a hard life but also were expressions of their joys, sorrows, hopes, and dreams for vindication and a better tomorrow.

In 1865 slavery was abolished in America. Fast-forward about 150 years, and today African Americans live in a free society. As a result of the sacrifices made by many people—both white and black—who fought for civil rights in America, African Americans and members of other minority groups have the legal right to enjoy the liberties this country was birthed on. All Americans have the right to own property, work, and make a decent living. Each of us has the right to pursue the American Dream.

Today, however, large numbers of U.S. citizens live at or below the poverty threshold, which means each day is a struggle to pay bills, provide for the basic needs of food, shelter, and clothing, and find access to health care. According to a report released by the U.S. Census Bureau, in 2005 there were approximately 37 million poor persons in America, many of them living in rural communities of the Deep South. Among them were 16 million people considered severely poor. These were families with two children and an annual income of less than $9,903—half the federal poverty level—trying to eke out an existence. The severely poor also include individuals trying to survive on less than $5,080 a year.[2] Considering the wealth of our nation, the fact that we would have even one family or individual living at this level of poverty in America is a shame.

In addition to the poverty problem, millions of people have difficulties managing debt. According to a survey conducted by Greenberg Quinlan Rosner Research, people recognize the seriousness of the debt issue and in particular identify debt as an obstacle for middle-class families. In fact, according to this same survey, people are more worried about falling into debt than about being the victim of a terrorist attack or natural disaster. Their concern reflects a personal experience with debt and a recognition of the challenges in today's economy.

In the twenty-first century we no longer have a system of slavery in America like the one that denied basic freedoms to my ancestors while generating financial wealth for the founders of our nation. However, there is an economic system at work whose cash flows of income and spending result in the unequal distribution of economic resources and the prevalent use of debt throughout our society. This system is producing a new type of "slave": the sort of person who helps to make up the working poor and debt-laden middle class. It is a system based on precepts and values that result in the rich getting richer while keeping goods, services, and other resources from reaching those who desperately need them.

In 2004 "the top 1 percent of households—719,910 of them, with an average income of $326,720—had almost 20 percent of the nation's pretax income, according to Kevin G. Hall of McClatchy Newspapers. This is up 17.8 percent since 2001. [Hall's] article reports the results of a study by UC Berkeley professor Emmanuel Saez. The research study also reports that the richest one-tenth of 1 percent of Americans—129,584 households in 2004—reported income equal to 9.5 percent of national pretax income."[3]

By contrast, in 2003 the Center for Budget and Policy Priorities reported that 13.1 million people, including 7.3 million children, lived in a "working-poor family," in which at least one adult was working yet unable to lift the family's income above the poverty line. "Thus about 50 million Americans do not make enough money to afford even the basics....The American Dream is no longer just being deferred; it is being eliminated for many people who work hard, play by the rules, and yet nonetheless see themselves falling further behind."[4]

This system also permits people to live way beyond their means by allowing them to finance out-of-control spending and greed-induced purchases with credit card and mortgage debt. "Household debt rose to 132 percent of disposable income [in 2005], partly because many Americans have pushed their credit card debt to the max and because many, including many high-income Americans, have piled on the mortgage debt. [In 2005], for the first time since the Depression, the personal savings rate for the nation fell below zero, meaning that Americans are spending more than they are earning (and are saving no money on a net basis)."[5]

The economic system I'm describing functions under the precept of the survival of the fittest, and therefore a natural consequence of the system is limited or no access by certain groups to the economic resources they need for daily living at the same time that others are accumulating abundant economic resources. But it's not just a systemic problem. Sometimes the people who are economically disenfranchised act in ways that keep them there, making their economic "slavery" that much worse.

The Bondage of the Oppressed

One's ability or lack of ability to create wealth can be a function of many factors, including personal ambition and ability, family history of wealth or poverty, quality of education, a changing job composition in society, offshoring of work, and even our federal tax structure. Some factors are considered "exogenous," meaning they are not within an individual's ability to control. Whether rich, poor, or in between, you can't control the family you were born into. You can carefully select the type of career you want and still find yourself unable to get a job because of a change in employment patterns in the community where you live. You can vote for legislators who share your ideology with regard to politics and taxation; however, no single individual can comprehensively affect our nation's tax laws. And you may be a member of a labor union, but when your employer makes a decision to send jobs overseas, you might find yourself out of a job. Nonetheless, there is one important factor that directly contributes to our ability to create wealth and that we can control. That's our attitude in response to the economic cards we've been dealt.

When economic winds shift and the climate gets cool, or when your inheritance and personal history don't look promising for wealth creation, you can choose to respond with courage or with cowardice. You can choose to walk by faith, develop a prosperous soul, and make decisions that reflect godly character, or you can have a defeatist attitude. Unfortunately, people who have been victimized by "the system" or who otherwise have gotten the short end of the economic stick are vulnerable to the most wealth-limiting factors in the world: a lack of vision, low self-worth, bitterness, and a bad attitude. Proverbs 29:18 says, "Where there is no vision, the people perish" (KJV). And indeed, when a lack of vision is mixed with low self-esteem, bitterness, and bad attitudes such as complacency and apathy, it colors people's mindset with hopelessness and causes them to embrace the victim role.

People with a victim mentality live with an expectation that someone else is going to help them. This expectation is so strong that they will actually refuse to take responsibility for their own actions, future, and finances. They are like the man who sat by the pool of Bethesda for thirty-eight years, waiting for someone to help him get into the pool (John 5:1-8). When Jesus saw his condition, he asked one simple but life-changing question: "Do you *want* to get well?" (verse 6; emphasis added).

The man's answer to Jesus' question was to begin explaining why his condition was a result of other people's behavior. "Sir," he said, "I have no one to help me into the pool when the water is stirred. While I am trying to get in, someone else goes down ahead of me" (verse 7).

I believe the man's answer annoyed Jesus. The Lord's response was to tell the man, "Get up!" (verse 8).

To his credit, the man did as he was ordered. And at once he was cured.

But note that, before the man could get up, he had to hear Jesus' words, believe in the vision Jesus cast, and then believe in himself. He had to give up being a victim. That's when he could embark on a new life of wholeness.

Changing our economic situation always begins with a decision to believe in ourselves and to deeply depend on ourselves to fulfill our God-given purpose. No one can ignore the fact that, like the historical slave trade system, today's free-market system divides economic masters from economic slaves, the hopeful from the hopeless, and the haves from the have-nots. But we have the power to make up in our own mind which side of the great divide we're going to live on and to take steps that move us in the direction where we want to go, regardless of where we start from.

With a positive mindset about who we are, the value God has placed on our lives, and a heart free from bitterness, we don't have to be the "slaves" of today's economy.

Opportunities along with the Problems

Economic masters own and control the wealth and knowledge that produce commerce in our free, global, and technology-driven marketplace. They are the providers of capital, the ones who rule over the distribution of economic resources. In other words, they create and control financial wealth.

Their depth of influence varies. Some masters control billion-dollar cash flows, while others control thousand-dollar cash flows. Oprah Winfrey and Bill Gates are economic "masters," but so are the small-business owners and marketplace workers who are able to make a living from their business, employee earnings, or other investments and owe no one anything.

Economic slaves, meanwhile, are consumers. They consume the goods and services that are the output of entities in the marketplace owned and controlled by the masters. To some extent, everyone is a consumer. But what distinguishes the consumption of a "slave" from the consumption of a "master," economically speaking, is that the slave consumes all he or she has, whereas the master does not. Indeed, this is what makes the former a slave.

Economic slaves receive capital via wages, payment transfers from the government, and borrowing, and they spend substantially all they receive. Economic masters, by contrast, take a portion of the income they receive and invest it in profit-producing assets, from which they earn more income. According to Proverbs 21:20, "In the house of the wise are stores of choice food and oil, but a foolish man devours all he has." Economic slaves in the world's system act foolishly, whereas economic masters apply knowledge, education, experience, and wisdom to create wealth.

There may be problems of unequal distribution of wealth and debt abuse associated with our economic system, but on the upside, this same system has created the largest economy in the world—the U.S. economy. According to the 2007 edition of *The Economist Pocket World in Figures*, for the year that ended December 31, 2004, the U.S. economy produced a gross domestic product (GDP) of $11,711.8 billion! By comparison, the second-largest economy was that of Japan, whose GDP was $4.622.8 billion for the same period. Also according to this source, U.S. business owners and entrepreneurs are the most creative and innovative people in the world. The U.S. infrastructure puts Americans at the top of the list in global competitiveness. Americans own three out of the top five largest companies in the world, and our nation is the second-largest exporter of goods and services. (The nations that comprise the Euro Area, as defined by *The Economist*, are number one in this category.)

The American economic system isn't perfect, but it *is* profitable. And for those who are willing and able to take advantage of it, it is the playground on which the game of wealth building is played out.

The Church and the Problems

Whatever a person's critique of the American economic system might be, and whether you're an economic master or an economic slave today, the fact remains that we live in the land of opportunity. So if people at the top of the food chain seem to flourish while the needs of hurting, helpless, or disenfranchised people seem to be ignored, then what should the church's response be?

Should we sit back and watch, letting worldly-minded people manage the situation?

Should poor Christians point fingers at the wealthy and those who are working hard to succeed in the marketplace, labeling them as the culprits? Or should rich Christians point fingers at the poor and say, "It's their own fault"?

Should church leaders describe big business and people desiring to make a profit as evil while exalting the poor? Or should pastors adopt a trickle-down approach to ministry, seeking to save the rich and then using the large offerings that result for local ministries and for feeding the poor?

Should the way the church demonstrates compassion for the poor be limited to giving them food and material resources, because that's the easiest thing to do?

Suppose poor Christians and community residents want to change their financial situation, but they simply don't know how to equip themselves for the marketplace and better manage their money. What should the church's response be?

Should church leaders promote a message that makes the rich feel guilty for being rich, or should they preach a message that promotes wealth creation for rich and poor alike?

Should the church try to impact personal and business economic development, or does this matter fall outside the scope of the church's responsibility?

What intervention is required of God's people when potentially harmful changes are occurring in our economy?

Tough questions, aren't they? But we can't dodge them. Remember, we are the church—the ministers of reconciliation and the people with good news.

Before an airplane takes off, flight attendants always give safety instructions. Included in those instructions are directions stating that, in case of an emergency, you are to put on your oxygen mask first, before you try to help someone else. That's because you can't help save someone else's life if you aren't able to sustain your own life.

Well, church, our country has an emergency: an economic one. As I've already demonstrated, poverty and debt are monumental problems that are only growing. But the situation is even worse than that. The emergency is the impending change in economic climate spurred by outsourcing, immigration, and international trade. Economic development in Asia and improvements in computer and communications technology have dramatically reduced the costs of international trade in goods and services. While these changes mean greater opportunities to create wealth for some, economists believe these factors will contribute to future wage inequality—the rich getting richer and the poor getting poorer—and impact the future economic well-being of middle- and lower-class Americans.[6] Suppose the recent trends of increasing wage inequality continue to the point where middle-class America as we've historically defined it no longer exists? Imagine a future like that.

The church is not, and will not be, exempt from the effects of forecasted changes on our economy. That's why I believe it is imperative for the church corporately, and for each Christian individually, to seize the opportunities highlighted by the changing economic climate in our nation and the world, and to practice the principles for creating eternal wealth. To the extent each Christian called by God to arise, go, and do increases his or her capacity to effectively make and manage financial resources, the church will be better positioned to respond to what are sure to be increasing opportunities to create wealth attributable to economic globalization and increasing levels of social needs due to wage inequality in America and poverty in the world.

Our God is the God of abundant life, and he delights in the prosperity of his people (Psalm 35:27). We should take advantage of our opportunity to prosper because God has a purpose for our prosperity: the creation of wealth—eternal wealth.

Purpose-Driven Prosperity

Prosperity begins with equipping ourselves to sustain our individual lives. But that is just the beginning. The purpose for prosperity goes beyond individual need and reaches to the combined needs of our families, the community, and the world we live in.

God doesn't give us the power to produce financial prosperity just so we can create wealth and live selfish, comfortable lives as individual "masters" in our world economic system. He gives us the power to produce wealth so that we can impact the world for righteousness and truth. God gives us the power to prosper so that we can be a blessing to someone else. He gives us the power to create wealth so that we can use our money, power, and influence to dominate and not be "slaves" to the kingdoms of this world—the kingdoms of business, technology, education, arts and entertainment, sports, politics and law, and health care.

We have a God-given purpose for our prosperity that is not self-centered. It is based on the Word of God, which says that we are to love other people just as we love ourselves. It is based on a spirit of giving and sharing. Like the young girl on the beach who chose to toss one starfish into the sea at a time (see chapter 7), an individual with a prosperous soul working hard to fulfill a God-inspired purpose can make a difference in a local, national, or global economic situation if that person is willing to share what he or she has with someone else.

Jesus said in Matthew 25:32-40 that the righteous are those who intervene when people are hungry or thirsty or in need of hospitality, clothing, healing, or a helping hand. Jesus wasn't talking about government intervention; he was talking about church intervention. If the effects of the inherent weaknesses of our economic system on the people in God's kingdom are going to be addressed, Christians must be at the forefront of that fight. But we can't begin to fight if we are impoverished or refuse to be generous, are motivated by greed and selfishness, or choose to serve the god of personal prosperity, just as do people in the world.

God established the church to be a beacon that is to shine brightly in the midst of increasing darkness. This means that, in addition to preaching the gospel of Jesus Christ, which has the power to save souls and to equip us for great financial success, the church must seek the answer to the following question: what are we to do about the problems of unequal distribution of resources, poverty, and injustice created by our world's economic system?

Finding the answer to this question is not a simple or one-dimensional task. The problem is complex, and likewise the solution will be complex. I wrote this book to introduce the principles for creating eternal wealth because I believe creating eternal wealth provides one answer to the question. The principles of stewardship introduced in part 1 form the framework for our wealth-creating efforts. Armed with the essentials for a prosperous soul, we have access to God's power and wisdom for creating wealth. Empowered by a God-inspired vision for our life and prosperity, we have a purpose for wealth that is elevated above the satisfaction of self-interest. We understand the problems as well as the opportunities created by the world's economic system. Now we need to get to work.

Getting to work means engaging in the elements of *purposeful and profitable action* that involve three things: (1) thinking and working like an entrepreneur, (2) strategically managing financial resources, and (3) building relationships and strategic alliances.

We'll be looking at these three parts of purposeful and profitable action in the following chapters. First though, in order to understand the importance of our work in the marketplace, it's important for us to understand that, according to the Scripture, we are all ministers.

Priests and Kings

In 2 Corinthians 5:17-18, 20, Paul says, "If anyone is in Christ, he is a new creation; old things have passed away; behold, all things have become new. Now all things are of God, who has reconciled us to Himself through Jesus Christ, and has given us the ministry of reconciliation.... Now then, we are ambassadors for Christ" (NKJV). Paul goes on to say in 2 Corinthians 6:4-5: "In all things we commend ourselves as ministers of God...[including] in labors" (NKJV). The Greek word translated "commend" is *sunistaö*, which means "to exhibit" or "to introduce." Even in our labors, the Scripture is saying, we are to exhibit, introduce, or carry ourselves as ministers of Christ.

From God's perspective, there is no division of labor and ministry: our labor is part of our ministry, and our ministry is in our labor. But is that how believers in today's church really act?

According to many churchgoers, Christians may be separated into two categories: "priests" (pastors) and "kings" (those working in the marketplace). People who espouse this theory believe the role of the pastor is to cast the vision for ministry, and the role of workers in the marketplace is to fund the vision through tithes and offerings.

The problem I have with this view is that it strips the role of minister (priest) from people who aren't called to pastor. Pastors are considered ministers, and ministers are New Testament priests. Therefore, if you aren't a pastor, then you're not a priest, and if you're not a priest, then you're not a minister.

But the Scripture doesn't make a distinction between ministers who work in a formal leadership position in the church and people who work in the marketplace. It says we are all ministers. As a matter of fact, Revelation 5:10 tells us we have been made kings and priests to serve our God. And so, again, there is no separation between our role as ministers unto God (priests) and our role as people called to dominate our field of influence in the marketplace (kings).

As you will see in the following chapters, engaging in purposeful and profitable action reconciles people's role as priest with their role as king or queen. Before the church can effectively engage in the battle against poverty and injustice, we have to understand who we are in Christ (priests of God) and know our position in Christ (kings and queens in the world).

Priests regularly come into the presence of God. Priests are knowledgeable about the Word of God. Priests are empowered by the anointing of God. Priests receive vision for their life and the lives of others from God.

Kings work and provide financial and material resources to sustain life. Kings fight battles against their enemies. Kings take care of their families and the people within their sphere of influence. Kings walk in wisdom, knowledge, and understanding.

People working in the marketplace can effectively commend themselves as ministers of God only if they embrace their role as priest *and* develop kingly abilities.

As we do our work, we must always remember that God has a purpose for our prosperity: He wants to position us for success in the marketplace so we can share good news with the lost, heal the brokenhearted, and set the captive free. The purpose for creating eternal wealth is not the same as the purpose most people have for wanting to achieve the American Dream. But when we create eternal wealth, it puts the church in a better position to respond to what are sure to be increasing levels of social and spiritual needs in our world. And it enables us to accrue benefits that will last forever.

It's time to turn our attention to engaging in purposeful and profitable action in the marketplace.

Questions for Reflection and Discussion

1. How would you compare and contrast living the American Dream with creating eternal wealth?

2. In addition to doing the work of an evangelist (God's mission of grace), what role do you think the church should play in fighting injustice and poverty?

3. Would you say your financial habits exhibit traits of an economic slave or those of an economic master?

4. How does your role as priest impact your work in the marketplace? How does your role as king impact your work in the church?

" People engaged in purposeful and profitable action create eternal wealth. "

Chapter 10

Purposeful and Profitable Action

I titled this book *Make Your Money Last Forever* because I know there are eternal consequences associated with how we create and manage wealth. Depending on how we choose to employ our time, abilities, and money, the blessing of working in a society where we are free to maximize our potential for creating wealth today may or may not produce results that benefit our eternity. As we explored in earlier chapters, if you want those benefits to last forever, you have to understand the principles of stewardship for creating eternal wealth and embark upon the amazing journey of strengthening your pillars of soul prosperity and God-inspired vision. These principles and two pillars work together to guide our efforts to create eternal wealth. They help us understand that our *being* in Christ must always precede our *doing* for Christ. And they remind us that there is a purpose for our prosperity. As seeking Christ first becomes the pattern for our approach to career success, we are in a place where God can bless us with increasing resources to manage for him.

When you think about the enormity of our world's economic and social challenges, and the continual effort it takes for the church to demonstrate God's love to hurting people, you quickly realize that as things get worse in the world, the church is going to need increasing numbers of competent, faith-filled people in the marketplace creating wealth and doing God's work. There is a cause-and-effect relationship at play here. Competent, faithful people attract increasing amounts of financial capital. Competent, faithful people earn increasing respect. Competent, faithful people are given increasing responsibilities, and as their responsibilities increase, so does their sphere of influence. Conversely, incompetent, unreliable people who lack commitment, focus, the right education, right attitude, relevant experience, and wisdom needed to generate creative solutions for marketplace challenges attract limited amounts of capital, respect, and influence.

Purposeful and profitable action incorporates the work we do in the marketplace in response to our understanding of God's purpose for our prosperity with the knowledge of who we are in Christ. When I use the term *work*, I mean devoting time and attention to serving the needs of stakeholders in the marketplace, such as employers, employees, coworkers, customers, suppliers, investors, and the government or other regulatory authorities to which we are accountable. I mean employing our gifts, skills, and abilities in the marketplace in exchange for tangible compensation. I also mean taking care of the money and other financial assets we're able to earn and control as a result of employing our services in the marketplace. Purposeful and profitable action focuses on the development of our capacity to creatively serve our gifts, skills, and abilities to the world, to steward financial and other resources we earn, and to work with others—all for the purpose of fulfilling our God-given destiny. Purposeful and profitable action produces eternal wealth.

There's Risk Associated with Wealth

Whenever you undertake the challenge of creating wealth, you assume some degree of risk. When you invest in the stock market, you're subject to the risk of declining stock prices. When you invest in real estate, you're subject to the risk of declining real estate values. When you invest in starting a new business, you're subject to the risk that it will fail. However, the risk of loss you are subject to is less than the potential for reward. Therefore, you take the risk in order to get the reward.

If creating wealth is a risky business, then creating eternal wealth is also a risky business. The risk we assume, however, is not limited to economic risk; it's also spiritual.

If we are successful in the marketplace but don't understand our God-given purpose, then when our ability to generate wealth takes us to greater levels of money, power, and prestige, we risk becoming a perpetrator of the problems identified with the world's economic and social systems instead of a part of the solution. We can become the one who uses money in a way that ignores the needs of the poor. We can become the one who makes business decisions that exploit people or harms our environment. We can become the one who neglects the responsibility of our marriage and/or family for the sake of career success. We can even be found guilty of violating the biblical principles for managing money for the sake of creating wealth. No one is exempt from the temptations of selfishness, greed, and pride associated with career success or owning and controlling material and financial resources. But we don't have to yield to such temptations. Thank God that he has given us the power to overcome them.

Keeping the seven stewardship principles for creating eternal wealth in the forefront of our minds, adding spiritual capital to our faith in increasing measure, and working to create *chayil* will help us overcome the temptations associated with making and managing money. This approach to creating wealth provides a framework for defining our priorities, values, goals, and wealth-creating strategies. It's that framework that distinguishes our efforts to succeed professionally from the world's efforts to get rich and that empowers us to prosper God's way. When we work within the confines of that framework, we can mitigate the risks associated with wealth and put ourselves in a position to boldly answer God's call to a marketplace ministry.

Calling All Entrepreneurs

After I left the corporate world at God's direction, my journey out of a lifestyle of seeking worldly wealth and prestige took four years. There was a lot of deadwood in my life to be pruned away, and I was living so deep in "Babylon" that I wasn't always an eager participant in the process. But I set my heart on seeking God's vision for my life after "Babylon." Like Jacob beside the Jabbok River (Genesis 32:22-26), I determined that I would not let go of God until he blessed me with his vision for my career and prosperity and his action plan for seeing the vision become real. As the months passed, God moved me to a place of total surrender and commitment to him, filling me with desire to perform his will in my life.

One of the most significant works God did in my life was to deepen my understanding of what he required of me as a wife and mother. I learned that being a businesswoman in the marketplace did not exempt me from following God's commands regarding a wife's attitude toward her husband. Married, working Christian women are to love and respect their husbands. Learning how to submit to our husbands and to love and respect them keeps our life in balance. As I began yielding to God's plan for the prosperity of my marriage, I began to experience the pleasant fruit that comes from doing what he says. Terence and I don't have a perfect marriage, but our relationship today is better than ever, partly because I am learning to live out God's pattern for me as a wife.

God also underscored to me that, for every working woman with children, motherhood is to be a greater priority than wealth or business success. My time off from pursuing a career corresponded with our son's teen years. I was able to focus my time and attention on Jonathan like I never could as a businesswoman working from dawn till dark every day. As I write this, Jonathan is eighteen years old, a freshman at the University of Washington, and a disciple of Jesus Christ. Putting my career on hold to learn God's valuable lessons about how to prosper as a mother by investing my life in raising our son is one of the greatest gifts I have ever received from God.

If you are a single parent or a working parent, you may be thinking, *That's great, Julaine, but I (we) have to work and raise my (our) children.* In that case my advice is to seek as much balance as you can between the demands of work and home. Try to find an employer who values family and is willing to allow flexibility in your work schedule. Become a master of time management. Discipline yourself to establish a schedule and then keep to that schedule. Include spending time with your children and going to school events in your schedule. Be willing to delay competing for a big promotion or more work responsibilities if that might cause you to lose time with your children and if you don't need the increased pay to live on.

Your time is the most important thing you can give your children, and choosing to give them that time is the key to your prosperity as a parent. Your children will be grown before you know it. When they leave your home and direct care, you'll have plenty of time to pour yourself back into your career. There's one thing about raising children that will never change: you don't get any do-overs.

As I poured my love into my husband and my home and worked my way through God's pruning, purging, and perfecting process, he finally birthed his new vision in my heart for my career. The vision came to me one day as I was in prayer. As the Lord met with me that day, he showed me an army of shackled and somewhat tattered and torn Christians. I heard God say, "My people are enslaved, working in businesses they neither own nor control or working for wages at or below poverty level. I want to bring them up and out of captivity. I want those who are earning low wages to be trained and equipped to increase their earnings. I'm calling out those in high-income jobs to begin entrepreneurial ventures that will benefit my kingdom." Then God revealed my divine assignment. He charged me with teaching people how to start their own businesses, run them with financial shrewdness, and improve their financial-management skills so they can create eternal wealth.

I'd been an employee my entire life. And now God was charging me to start a business. The assignment was intimidating. However, I knew that my life experiences had prepared me to answer the call. That's how God works. He doesn't waste any of our experiences; instead, he uses them to prepare us to fulfill our destiny.

Just as God birthed a vision in my heart for the work I was to do in the marketplace, he will do the same for you, if he hasn't already done so. Your purpose and vision will most likely look completely different from mine. But they will reveal God's designated plan for you to create eternal wealth benefiting his kingdom.

You'll need to arm yourself with the framework of God's stewardship principles, a prosperous soul, and God-inspired vision as you embark upon your journey. And you'll need to prepare yourself to work in ways you never dreamed of. That's because there's no doubt that God's plan will require you to do work that will ultimately result in your meeting the tangible needs of others in ways you never imagined. Call it your *soul plan*.

The Entrepreneur's Soul Plan Is Her Marketplace Ministry

Entrepreneurs are risk takers. They pursue their purpose with passion and assume business and economic risk for the sake of fulfilling that purpose and creating wealth. From an eternal wealth perspective, however, being an entrepreneur who starts a business or a new career is not about trying to get rich; it is about answering a clarion call to fulfill our kingdom assignment in the marketplace. Our kingdom assignment in the marketplace is what I term our *soul plan*.

I have defined *soul plan* as a practical, work-related plan of action to employ our gifts, skills, and abilities in the marketplace in a manner that fulfills God's purposes. Once you discover what God wants you to do in the marketplace, you have to act to fulfill that purpose. Your plan of action is your soul plan. Why do I call it a soul plan? Because whenever God gives us a marketplace assignment, the purpose will always be to serve the needs of others, thereby impacting their lives for the sake of his kingdom.

A soul plan will engage you in work that impacts the lives of people to whom you provide services. But since individuals comprise work groups, departments, companies, markets, and even economies, a soul plan can have broader influence than its effects on an individual.

On a corporate or global level, soul plans are intended to change the environment in which business is done on the earth. Soul plans are to establish the marketplace of God's kingdom on the earth. To that end, God is revealing soul plans to his people throughout the earth. That is why he said to me that he wanted his people trained to earn higher incomes and that he wanted high-income earners to start their own businesses. God wants his church better positioned to address the current and future challenges arising from the world's economic system. And what better way to establish the marketplace of his kingdom than by giving people in the body of Christ a vision for their careers that will bring them out of captivity to the world's system? But don't make the mistake of responding to your soul plan by fixating on how to get rich. That's the wrong focus.

I made that mistake. After God revealed my soul plan to me, the first thing I did was ask him to give me a revenue plan for my business.

A revenue plan is that part of a business plan that outlines the business's revenue sources. Based on my years of corporate finance and operations experience, I knew that every good business plan must be built on a solid revenue-generating plan. Revenue drives cash flow, and cash flow pays bills. However, my fixation on money and wanting to increase my income led me to ask God the wrong question. He wasn't interested in giving me a revenue plan per se, because he knew that wasn't what I needed to get started. He *was* interested, however, in my fully understanding my *soul plan* and discovering how to actualize it, developing the skills, abilities, and products or services that would satisfy the needs of the people God was calling me to serve. Soul plans focus on serving people, not making money.

Executing a soul plan begins with understanding our purpose. Then it extends to understanding the needs or desires of our current or potential employers or customer target market. Once we understand those needs, we can connect them to our gifts, skills, and abilities. But unless we become people focused and stop fixating on money, we will not be able to develop the plan of action that we need to get the job done.

God knows more about business than we do, and so he also knows that it takes money to make money and that in business cash is king: no cash means no business. Soul plans don't ignore economics. But in the marketplace of God's kingdom, Jesus is the King of kings. And Jesus cares about meeting the needs of people. Therefore, when he gives us a soul plan, it's because he wants us to do something on the earth that will positively impact our lives and the lives of others for the sake of his kingdom. And he expects us to work in a manner that will bring glory to God. Therefore, while we shouldn't ignore economics in soul plans, our focus must first be on people and on fulfilling God's purposes as we serve people. God knew I would not discover how to actualize my soul plan if my focus started and stayed on money. He also knew that once I actualized my soul plan, the money would come.

A soul plan operates on two dimensions, those of the marketplace and the church. From both a marketplace and a church perspective, a soul plan is a powerful expression of your mission that draws your attention away from money. It expresses your opportunity to serve your gifts, skills, and abilities to the world. It connects your purpose to the fulfillment of work *God* wants done in the marketplace, which means it also connects your purpose to the mission of the church in the marketplace. A soul plan is a business or career plan for serving your gifts, skills, and abilities to the marketplace in a manner that fulfills your purpose, benefits the kingdom of God, and creates eternal wealth.

When we execute a soul plan, we embark upon a journey that capitalizes on our greatest asset: being our authentic self. A soul plan erases any guilt or fear we may have because of our ambitious career goals or desire to win in the game of business. God wants us to have successful careers and to win whatever game he calls us to play, even the game of business! A soul plan releases us to pursue our careers and entrepreneurial ventures without hesitation or any questions about whether God wants us to succeed in the marketplace. A soul plan is our insurance that when all is said and done, we will not find out we ran the wrong race. That's because following our soul plan enables us to be true to ourselves and obedient to God. It will always engage us in performing the work he prepared in advance for us to do (Ephesians 2:10).

You won't have to force yourself to develop the passion to work your soul plan; you'll want to work it. Your passion will spring forth from your vision, and your vision will be generated from your unique purpose, the one God gave you. Consequently, you will be doing something you love and you will be good at it. Like every good entrepreneur, you'll assume the risks associated with changing a career or starting a business because the promised rewards associated with fulfilling God's plan for your life are far greater than the risks you'll assume.

Not so sure you have a soul plan? Oh yes, you do.

The Character of an Entrepreneur

In his book *E-Myth Mastery*, entrepreneur and popular business speaker Michael Gerber states, "Each of us is born with the inherent impulse, a creative center, which when cultivated through disciplined learning and practice, can produce works in the world that defy the imagination."[1]

Gerber's assertion reflects the biblical truth that we are all made in the image of God. Human beings have a "creative center" because we are the handiwork of *the* Creator. Therefore, when we connect our inborn creativity to God through faith in Jesus Christ, our ability to create soars beyond anything we can do for selfish gain to wonderful things we do through the power of God to benefit his kingdom. Entrepreneurship doesn't require business ownership. It requires that we think creatively about how to fulfill our God-given purpose and be willing to take risks and to work hard. Eternally successful entrepreneurship in God's kingdom results when people allow God's power to energize their creative capacity so that their skills are actualized at a level of effectiveness that produces outstanding results in the marketplace. To put it another way, a successful entrepreneur knows how to think creatively, behave wisely, and do work that matters. What is work that matters? Work that fulfills our soul plan.

Researchers have studied the personalities of successful people, trying to identify those traits they could term *entrepreneurial*. Of course the question people want answered is, are entrepreneurial characteristics natural or learned? Based on my years of work experience, I believe the answer is both. I believe that entrepreneurial behavior is akin to leadership. Having been trained in Dr. Myles Munroe's school of servant leadership, I also believe that inside every follower is a leader waiting to get out and that each of us is born to lead in our unique area of gifting. Leadership develops as we serve our unique gifts and abilities to the world. And we serve our gifts and abilities to the world by meeting the needs of others.

Entrepreneurial behavior is simply a manifestation of our servant leadership. Therefore, some characteristics are a reflection of our unique personality and gifting, and some are the result of learned behaviors. And since entrepreneurship is at least in part a skill that can be learned, the rest of this chapter is designed to teach you how you can become an entrepreneur—or how to become a better one, if you are already engaged in entrepreneurial work. I hope that as you read through my description of entrepreneurship you'll find it helpful in your quest to serve the needs of others and fulfill your soul plan.

To begin, let's consider a category of workers you may never have thought could be entrepreneurs.

Entrepreneurial Managers

Entrepreneurs are typically thought to be people who organize, operate, and assume risk for a business venture. However, I think people who are servant leaders and who use their creative abilities to help their employers manage organizations, product lines, or services and achieve their business objectives are also entrepreneurs. I call these people *entrepreneurial managers*.

Entrepreneurial managers are people who are empowered by a clear, God-inspired vision that puts them in a position to work for someone else. Their desire to please God as well as their employer drives them to work at the highest level of their capacity. Because entrepreneurial managers have vision, they also tend to be optimistic. They are industrious and never afraid of hard work.

Entrepreneurial managers are self-appointed.

Since, by definition, entrepreneurial managers are people empowered by their God-inspired vision to work at the highest level of their capacity and fulfill their soul plan, being an entrepreneurial manager is not something you achieve when you get a management job for a corporation. You achieve the status of entrepreneurial manager when you discover your soul plan and begin to think creatively and act wisely to execute that plan. Entrepreneurial managers are empowered by a passion to fulfill their work-related purpose as revealed to them by God. Being an entrepreneurial manager is a matter of your mindset, not your position on a company's organization chart.

Entrepreneurial managers are continual learners.

Entrepreneurial managers seize opportunities to learn as much as they can about their trade, employer's business, and industry, no matter what position they hold in the company. For example, your job may be to bag groceries at a supermarket. But if you're an entrepreneurial manager, you'll have a desire to learn something more about how a supermarket is run. In addition to doing a great job bagging groceries for customers, your entrepreneurial spirit might cause you to take the initiative to learn how the store manager reorders and controls inventory. To take another example, you may be hired to work in the mail room of a large corporation. If you're an entrepreneurial manager in this position, not only will you do a great job sorting and delivering mail, but you also will take the initiative to learn something about the work that is done in different departments of your company. Or maybe you already run a department or division. If you're an entrepreneurial manager, you won't just pay attention to what's going on in the work groups under your authority. You'll also pay general attention to what's going on in your company, its industry, and the global economy and use that information to help your company succeed. Entrepreneurial managers are people whose vision for their future and passion to fulfill their soul plan inspires them to be continual learners.

Entrepreneurial managers are change agents.

Entrepreneurial managers are mavericks with regard to their vision and creative-thinking abilities. They look at rules, systems, and ways of doing things (also known as the status quo) as suggestions. They don't think of themselves as being above the rules; however, they are constantly looking for a better way of doing things. When an entrepreneurial manager notices inefficiencies or waste in a process, she will think of ways to increase efficiencies or eliminate waste and will share her ideas about that with her supervisor. An entrepreneurial manager can see things that others don't: empowered by God's Spirit, she has "super" vision. She is able to identify ways to improve business processes and she is willing to share those ideas with others.

Entrepreneurial managers aren't just ingenious (seeing a better way of doing something); they are also innovative (able to execute a plan to do something better). They exercise sound judgment and make good decisions. They see work-related problems as challenges and see challenges as opportunities to make a difference in the workplace.

Entrepreneurial managers have integrity and work well with others.
Entrepreneurial managers are usually great networkers. Even when they are not formal leaders in an organization, they're able to exercise positive influence within the organization through informal networking channels.

Entrepreneurial managers operate with integrity: they tell the truth and they keep their word. And while their entrepreneurial nature causes them to be great change agents, they adhere to their company's policies and the laws and regulations of governing authorities, with respect to both the letter of the law and the spirit of the law. And entrepreneurial managers take responsibility for their actions, including their mistakes. When they make a mistake, they work hard to fix it.

Entrepreneurial managers advance through an organization.
The approach such managers take to work often produces excellent results.

Their competent work and optimistic attitude make them candidates for bonuses and promotions. That's because companies often reward and promote employees who demonstrate these traits and help management get the job done.

During my years of working in corporate finance and operations, I had the opportunity to reward many people with bonuses and promotions. Based on that experience, I developed the following framework to help me identify employees who were ready for promotion or who deserved a performance bonus. As you read through these points, you'll notice that in almost every case the performance trait can be linked back to a trait of an entrepreneurial manager. Individuals who receive bonuses or promotions demonstrate the following:

- Competency in their current role
- An ability to perform at the next level
- A proven track record of contributing to the company's efforts to solve problems and meet its objectives
- Strong leadership potential
- An ability to make tough decisions
- High energy and enthusiasm about their job and the company
- Optimism and an ability to get the job done under pressure

I'm not suggesting that if you think and work like an entrepreneurial manager and demonstrate the traits listed above you'll automatically receive a bonus or promotion from your employer. I can, however, guarantee that if you learn to do these things you will improve your chances of having your name on the top of the list of employees who deserve a bonus when bonuses are paid. You will also improve your chances of being identified by management as someone to groom for next-level responsibilities. And consequently, you will increase your influence and earnings in the company you work for. Why is this important? Because as your ability to influence others and your income increases so does the scope of your soul plan.

Other traits of entrepreneurial managers.
Let me offer a few more words of advice about the character of an entrepreneurial manager. Each of these is both a practical and a spiritual point to bear in mind.

First, don't hang your entrepreneurial manager attitude on the hook of an agenda to get promoted or be noticed. People can tell whether your work effort is authentic or motivated by selfishness and a desire for attention.

Second, if you get passed over for a promotion, raise, or bonus, don't develop a negative attitude. Your work will continue to speak for you if you place a guard over your attitude and remain positive.

Third, promote a team environment by working well with other people. You don't need to isolate yourself for your work to stand out. In fact, the opposite is true. As you promote effective teamwork within your work group, you'll draw more attention to your willingness to serve the needs of others for the sake of achieving a group objective. Servant leaders are people who inspire and influence others to reach their potential, so when you promote teamwork, you demonstrate servant leadership.

Fourth, remain humble in the face of accolades and praise for a job well done. Prideful and arrogant behavior or attitudes will isolate you from your coworkers (because people won't like you), lead to division within the work group (because people won't like you), are usually not tolerated by upper management (because people won't like you), and will diminish your chances of promotion in most organizations (because people won't like you). Get the picture? How can you execute your soul plan if people don't like you or want to work with you?

Remember, in addition to your desire to please your employer, your motivation for doing a great job at work should include a desire to please God. he hates pride and arrogance (Proverbs 6:17; 8:13; 16:18; 29:23). In God's kingdom humility precedes honor (Proverbs 15:33; 18:12).

Finally, stay out of cliques and groups where people groan and complain about the company or their jobs. It's almost impossible to change someone's opinion about you once you damage your reputation in the workplace by aligning yourself with people who are pessimistic and constantly on a soapbox complaining about something at work. Avoid these people! Aligning yourself with them will not increase your chances of advancement, because management is not going to promote a troublemaker. And whether it's warranted or not, people who complain all the time are considered by management to be troublemakers. Furthermore, if you hang around people like this long enough, their bad attitude will begin to rub off on you. "Bad company corrupts good character" (1 Corinthians 15:33).

What does all this have to do with your soul plan? I think the answer is *everything*. Doing excellent work opens doors for you to influence the way work gets done. And when you have the power to influence the way works get done, you can impact the marketplace for the sake of God's kingdom. Adopting the traits of an entrepreneurial manager and doing an excellent job for your employer is your marketplace ministry; it's an expression of your soul plan. Excellent work keeps you from putting your ministry to shame and will enable you to stand before great men and women (Proverbs 22:29 NKJV). And, if God gives you the vision, such work prepares you to take the next step in eternal-wealth-creating entrepreneurship: business ownership.

Preparation to Be a Business Owner

Whether you continue to work as an employee, or whether God's calling you to advance to business ownership, being an entrepreneurial manager will help you generate financial resources for creating eternal wealth. As an employee, you enjoy the benefits of increasing salary and compensation levels when you think and act like an entrepreneurial manager. But the money you make, the lessons you learn, and the relationships you build during your years of experience as an entrepreneurial manager also prepare you for successful business ownership.

The process of starting a new business is complex, and I'm not going to fully examine that process in this book. If God is calling you to start a new business, you'll want to do some business planning and market research to get started. I've included some books and resource materials in the recommended reading list at the end of the book to help you in that regard. Having gone through the transition from employee to business owner, I understand how intimidating the process can be. I'm going to share what I have learned about the transition in hopes that this information will help you get comfortable with the notion that you can start your own business.

Successful business ownership begins with education and experience. Many successful entrepreneurs who are business owners start out as employees. In fact, the work they do as an employee often serves as a platform from which they can leap to the level of business ownership.

Education and work experience are a breeding ground from which actionable business ideas are birthed. Education equips you with the skills to get your first job. Once you land your first job and embark on your career, God will use the work experience and education you obtain to help you discover the new business idea he wants you to pursue.

Pino Audia and Chris Rider, two researchers from the Haas School of Business at the University of California–Berkeley explored the notion that entrepreneurs are actually "organizational products." According to their theory, entrepreneurs are more likely to be people who were employed by existing organizations than individuals who never worked for someone else.[2] Their study makes the point that when people work for a business it builds their confidence to start another business, gives them knowledge and detailed information about potential new business ideas, and helps them form the social network they'll need for the new business. Working for someone else prepares you to handle the responsibilities associated with working for yourself or starting a company.

We all love to hear tales about a groundbreaking innovation that was started in a basement, garage, or dorm room by a smart and energetic young entrepreneur. In these stories we marvel at how a seemingly ordinary person is able to come up with a brilliant idea that revolutionizes the marketplace and generates large amounts of money for the fortunate founder. Stories like those of Bill Hewlett and David Packard, who started a computer company in their garage, of Michael Dell, who started another such company in his dorm room, and of Bill Gates, who dropped out of college and started Microsoft in his garage, inspire us and remind us that the American Dream can be achieved. While I grant that each of these guys' businesses started with an idea and they were able to build huge, profitable enterprises from that idea, keep in mind that in every case they also had enough prior education to conceive the idea in the first place.[3]

Your education will prepare you to start a new business, just like Hewlett and Packard's, Dell's, and Gates's education helped prepare them to start their companies. You may not have the opportunity to attend an Ivy League university to obtain that education; however, your work experience can be a powerful and effective educator, preparing you to transition from your role as entrepreneurial manager to business owner.

Successful business owners are self-starters.
Making the change from being an employee to starting a business is not

easy. While your work experience and education go a long way toward preparing you for this step, you'll need new skills and abilities as well. One of the biggest challenges you'll face as you transition from being an employee to starting a company is learning to stop thinking like a manager.

As an manager, you planned strategies to meet already identified objectives, organized resources (human, financial, and material) to carry out someone else's strategy, and controlled the use of those resources to ensure they were put to the best use vis-à-vis your employer's budget and objectives. But starting a company means there are no people or processes to manage. You have to set up the operations. You have to create the processes. And even if you have business partners, until you develop your processes and hire your first employees there won't be any employees or processes to manage except yourself. You have to be a self-starter.

When you transition to being a business owner, you have to create the business strategy; you have to secure the cash to pay the bills; and then you have to pay the bills. You have to do the hands-on detailed work that every start-up requires. You have to design and document the business processes. You have to develop the product or services. You have to hire the employees. You have to develop your customer base. You have to take on your competitors. And you have to position (and reposition) the company to ensure its fiscal and operational effectiveness. You are the source of direction, vision, goal setting, and innovation for your company. You have to inspire and motivate yourself.

Successful business owners scale down to build up.

New business owners must learn how to scale down to do a start-up. As an employee working for an established enterprise, you were used to having access to the financial, technical, human, and material resources you needed to do your job. As a start-up, chances are you won't have access to the same level of resources you did when you worked for an established enterprise, but you still have to get the job done. And here's the catch: you have to do it with just as good or better quality results.

My biggest frustration during my transition period has been my lack of readily available computer tech support. I never had to be self-sufficient with regard to the computer because during my career I always had access to a skilled IT department staff. Whenever I needed anything, an IT staff person was available to get it or fix it. Today, when I need computer support, I have one of two choices: (1) get it myself, or (2) fix it myself. Notice the common denominator: myself. Even when the problem is so bad that I have to hire a technician to fix it, I look over his or her shoulder so that if the problem ever happens again, perhaps I'll be able to fix it or get what I need without having to call a techie.

Again, the point I'm making is this: be ready to scale down your approach to operating your company, but don't sacrifice the quality of your work in the process. And that's what makes starting a new business so challenging. When people say, "I want to start a business so I'll have more free time," I know they don't understand what they're talking about. Starting a new business is like having a new baby. You don't get more free time; you lose time. Your business needs your constant care and attention during its infant and toddler years (roughly the first five years of its life).

Successful business owners are committed to their success.
Your level of commitment to your business's success has to be deep enough to get you through the tough times. No matter how sure you are that you're doing the right thing at the right time in response to God's direction, the day will come when doubt will cloud your mind. You'll question your decision to start the business. It's at this time that you'll need the support of your family and the friends you trust.

Fortunately, when you are doing work based on an understanding of your purpose and to execute your soul plan, then your passion will give you the conviction to carry on no matter what. Conviction is a strong belief. Conviction births perseverance. Having a strong belief in your purpose, and knowing that God prepared in advance for you to do this work (Jeremiah 29:11; Ephesians 2:10), will strengthen your conviction and enable you to persevere during the tough times.

Successful business owners sell value-added products.
As you become increasingly familiar with your business idea and are certain that God is calling you to start a business, you'll begin working through the process of developing your product or service. At this point it is important to keep in mind that successful ideas for a new business must be actionable and add value to the marketplace. Actionable, value-added business ideas are ideas that will solve a problem or satisfy a desire of a specific target market. Don't make the mistake of assuming that the product you love to make or the service you enjoy rendering represents a viable business opportunity. Or that you will sell your product to everyone. Just because you're passionate about something doesn't make it a good business idea. And not everyone is going to buy your product.

Following are some questions for you to answer as you assess whether your business idea is actionable and adds value to the marketplace (when I use the word *product*, I mean both products and services):

1. Is there an established market for your product?
2. If there isn't an established market for your product, is there an identifiable economic or market trend that you are confident you can exploit to create a demand for your product? (If you answered question 1 with no and question 2 with yes, keep in mind that you are banking on a strategy that says, "Build it and

they will come." This business strategy is inherently risky, and therefore your business plan should be based on thorough market research and include specific tactics to mitigate that risk. Also, be extremely conservative when planning operating revenues for the first few years.)

3. Who is the specific target market for your product?
4. What is the value-added characteristic of your product (i.e., how is it faster, better, or cheaper than what your competitor offers)?
5. How is your product differentiated from that of your competitors?
6. How will you get your product to your customer?
7. How will your product satisfy customer needs and wants?
8. How does the product work?
9. Will your product save your customers time or money?
10. Will your product generate more profits for your customers?

The product or service has to be something that other people either need or desire. No matter how much you love it, if your customers don't need or want it, you don't have a sustainable business idea. This is true for for-profit as well as nonprofit businesses. In the case of a nonprofit, the idea must solve a problem or satisfy a desire that is shared by members of the community the nonprofit will serve. In the case of a for-profit enterprise, the idea usually involves delivering innovative products or services that fulfill a desire or help people do something better, faster, or cheaper. Carefully assess the added value of your product and work through the process of solidifying your business idea.

Successful business owners take time to plan.

Being in a hurry to open a new business or launch a new product is not smart. In the heyday of the dot-com boom, the conventional wisdom held that you should enter a market before you had finished surveying the competitive landscape, identified the right opportunity, and designed a compelling strategy. The proponents of this strategy believed the notion that you have to act now; you can't afford to think about it. Now that many dot-com start-ups have collapsed, this wisdom is being challenged. Industry studies are concluding that moving fast to market should not be an excuse for shortchanging the business planning process. Studies prove that making a decision to move fast to market at the expense of completing a thorough business plan and gathering the right resources rarely pays off.[4]

> **Ten Keys for Managing Economic and Business Risk**
>
> 1. Do what it takes to live a balanced, prioritized lifestyle. Put God first, family second, and business third.
> 2. Develop a support network of family and friends; you'll need it to lean on.
> 3. Identify economic and business risks, but focus on the upside. Remain optimistic.
> 4. Make sure you possess the requisite skills and experience to succeed before you start the business.
> 5. Business may be risky, but put forth the effort and go for your dream. The greater risk is to give up or not try at all.
> 6. Start with a great, actionable business idea—an idea that the market values.
> 7. Obtain the right financial backing.
> 8. Attract, manage, and retain the right people.
> 9. Read business books, magazines, and periodicals to stay abreast of changes in the local, national, and global business environment.
> 10. Continually innovate and increase your knowledge. You can reduce risk with information and practice.

Today's entrepreneur has to balance the benefits and risks of moving fast. The good news for God-inspired entrepreneurs is that God will help us perfect our timing if we commit our work to him (Proverbs 16:3, 9). He has a way of using issues, events, and people to slow down, speed up, or otherwise adjust our timing. And with his timing, we will be able to survive and thrive in a challenging economy, helping to work his will in the world.

Successful business owners manage risk.
It should be evident at this point that entrepreneurs manage business and economic risks when creating eternal wealth. There's no such thing as a bored God-inspired entrepreneur. Creating and producing products or services—and doing it better, faster, and cheaper than large corporations—is exhilarating. Add to that the joy and excitement associated with doing anything for God, and you're in for a wild wide. It's like riding a roller coaster: scary and fun at the same time. The risks are great, but so are the rewards.

Putting It All in Perspective

Whether you're an entrepreneurial manager or an entrepreneur running a business, entrepreneurship could be the means for you to wage a war against the downside effects of our changing economy. In fact, according to Carl Schramm (president of the Kauffman Foundation, the world's leading foundation for enterepreneurship), entrepreneurship could be the force most likely to provide true freedom for individuals across the globe and in America by giving everyone the opportunity to fulfill their potential.[5] Imagine what the results would be if a spirit of entrepreneurship began to flourish throughout the churches in America. Imagine what could happen if God-inspired people began to pursue new business ideas or grab hold of new visions for how to maximize their potential as entrepreneurial managers.

I believe that when God told me that he wanted people working in low-income jobs to develop their skills so they could increase their earning potential, and that he was calling his people out from their high-income positions to start entrepreneurial ventures, he was also revealing what the next move of his Spirit would be in the church. He was revealing his plan for expanding the wealth-creating capacity of his church for the purpose of financing the end-time harvest and impacting the needs of a hurting world by releasing our entrepreneurial capacity. In the process, people would also be freed from the bondage of financial slavery. I believe God is calling people to be strong and courageous, to retool, and in some cases to redeploy themselves and their wealth in order to produce more wealth.

The Scriptures promise that when we delight in the law of God and meditate on that law day and night, whatever we do will prosper (Psalm 1). As Christians who trust God and are seeking first his kingdom and his righteousness, we have the right to boldly approach his throne and to ask him to give us the desires of our heart, to make all our plans succeed, and to grant all our requests (Psalm 20:4-5). We have something the world doesn't have: a relationship with God through Jesus Christ, which empowers us to do great exploits to the glory of God. We have an ability to see the future more clearly than others do, because what eyes have not seen, what ears have not heard, and what has not entered into the minds of men and women God reveals to us by his Spirit (1 Corinthians 2:9). When we begin executing our soul plan by deploying ourselves into our careers, understanding that our ministry is in our labor, not only can we produce additional wealth but we also can impact the marketplace for the sake of the gospel. And most important, we position ourselves to help others do the same thing. What a privilege to be used by God in such an awesome way!

Entrepreneurship in response to the visions God gives to us, if we are obedient and prudent in responding to him, will lead to wealth. But it's the uses of our wealth that makes it *eternal* wealth and not just temporal wealth. That's what we will explore in the next chapter.

Questions for Reflection and Discussion

1. To what degree are you serving your gifts, skills, and abilities in the marketplace?

2. What motivates you to go to work each day? If your motivation isn't to execute your soul plan, what changes do you need to make to be able to work at that level?

3. List those things you should do more of or stop doing in order to maximize the effectiveness of your work as an entrepreneur.

4. Do you think wanting power in the marketplace is a good or a bad thing, and why?

" Generous giving opens doors

to eternal dwelling places. "

Chapter 11

STRATEGICALLY MANAGING FINANCIAL RESOURCES

In the last chapter I talked about purposeful and profitable action in the marketplace. Purposeful and profitable action connects the work we do as priests to our role as kings and queens. One aspect of that work involves assuming the risks and rewards of entrepreneurship. Engaging in entrepreneurship is the way we execute our soul plan.

As our competency in doing entrepreneurial work increases, so do our income and influence in the marketplace. How we choose to use our income and influence contributes directly to our ability to create eternal wealth.

If you knew that the degree to which you used your money to serve the needs of other people as you served God was the same degree to which you would be welcomed into eternal habitations, would it affect the way you spend your money today? I think most people would answer this question with a yes. Jesus made an interesting correlation between the reception we'll receive into eternal dwelling places and the way we use our money today when he told the parable of the unjust manager.

Jesus told his disciples: "There was a rich man whose manager was accused of wasting his possessions. So he called him in and asked him, 'What is this I hear about you? Give an account of your management, because you cannot be manager any longer.'

"The manager said to himself, 'What shall I do now? My master is taking away my job. I'm not strong enough to dig, and I'm ashamed to beg—I know what I'll do so that, when I lose my job here, people will welcome me into their houses.'

"So he called in each one of his master's debtors. He asked the first, 'How much do you owe my master?'

" 'Eight hundred gallons of olive oil,' he replied.

"The manager told him, 'Take your bill, sit down quickly, and make it four hundred.'

"Then he asked the second, 'And how much do you owe?'

" 'A thousand bushels of wheat,' he replied.

"He told him, 'Take your bill and make it eight hundred.'

"The master commended the dishonest manager because he had acted shrewdly. For the people of this world are more shrewd in dealing with their own kind than are the people of the light. I tell you, use worldly wealth to gain friends for yourselves, so that when it is gone, you will be welcomed into eternal dwellings." (Luke 16:1-9)

The unjust manager's poor track record got him fired. The only clue we have concerning the nature of his performance deficiency is that he wasted his master's possessions. (Sounds like the third servant in the parable in Matthew 25.) What I find interesting about this parable is why the master would fire the manager for wasting his assets and then commend him for his obviously dishonest behavior. What did the manager do that the master found worthy of praise?

He thought strategically. And it was his strategic thinking and use of money to benefit his future that earned his master's praise. The wise thing the manager did was use money to serve the needs of others for his benefit. In that regard he was both diligent and industrious as he engaged in the strategic use of money for the benefit of his future dwelling place.

The manager's goal was clear: he had to find a new place to live and work that would keep him from begging and digging. His strategy was simple: involve his master's debtors by appealing to their greed, thereby cultivating a shared sense of benefit in the deal. His execution was flawless: he acted authoritatively and quickly. The effective implementation of his strategy hinged on a common quid pro quo maneuver—you scratch my back and I'll scratch yours.

After Jesus told this parable, he made the following statement: "The people of this world are more shrewd in dealing with their own kind than are the people of the light. I tell you, use worldly wealth to gain friends for yourselves, so that when it is gone, you will be welcomed into eternal dwellings" (Luke 16:8-9). Jesus wasn't exalting the manager's behavior to suggest that we should try to make friends by behaving unscrupulously to gain financial wealth for our benefit and theirs. The message Jesus hid in this parable was intended to give us the strategy for how to use our money today for the benefit of our future dwelling place. Jesus gave us the financial strategy for creating eternal wealth.

God's Financial Strategy for Creating Eternal Wealth

If you look up the word *strategy* in a business text, you'll find a definition that reads something like this: "Strategy: a blueprint of all the important entrepreneurial, competitive, and functional area actions that are to be taken in pursuing organizational objectives and positioning the organization for sustained success."[1] A strategy is a game plan to achieve a specific goal. Before you can act strategically on any matter, you have to do the following:

1. Establish your long-term goal.
2. Set specific performance objectives to achieve your long-term goal.
3. Formulate strategies to achieve your objectives.
4. Develop tactics to execute the strategies.

Applying this definition, then, a financial strategy for creating eternal wealth is a set of entrepreneurial, competitive, and disciplined actions that an individual takes in pursuing personal financial objectives and positioning himself or herself for sustained eternal success.

Before we talk about some of the actions you can take to implement your financial strategy for creating eternal wealth, I want to review some key concepts we've learned thus far about how to make your money last forever.

First, all our wealth-creating endeavors should be built upon the foundation of the seven eternal wealth principles taken from the parable of the three servants (see chapter 2). Those principles remind us that we are stewards of every resource on earth and accountable to God for how we use those resources.

Second, God has a plan for the distribution of goods and services that will achieve his purposes. God's purpose is to take care of his family and fulfill the mission of his enterprise, which is to spread the gospel of Jesus Christ throughout the world.

Third, there is another system competing for our allegiance: the system for creating worldly wealth. When we make financial decisions guided by the invisible hand of self-interest instead of God's invisible hand, then we cross the line dividing the pathway for creating eternal wealth from the pathway for creating worldly wealth.

Fourth, developing a prosperous soul, understanding our purpose, and conceiving a vision for our work life through intimacy with God creates a framework for our wealth creating efforts.

Fifth, as members of the church, we have been commissioned by Jesus to spread the good news of God's kingdom throughout the world. Fulfilling the Great Commission requires that we get involved in the fight against poverty and injustice. That is why it's important for us to maximize our influence in the marketplace by maximizing our effectiveness in the marketplace.

Last, executing our soul plan by engaging in purposeful and profitable action is possible as an entrepreneurial manager or a business owner.

Developing a Financial Strategy for Creating Eternal Wealth

Every person has a goal for managing finances and an internal agenda for executing it. Sometimes our goals are long term, well thought through, and explicitly stated in the form of a budget, savings, investment, or retirement plan. Sometimes they are short-sighted, impulsive, and implicit, such as choosing to ignore money matters or spending money we don't have by purchasing things on credit. Whether they are explicit or implicit, our money-management strategies affect our ability to achieve our financial goals.

Typically, people's strategies for managing their finances focus on achieving temporal goals. They want to buy a home or car, pay for a child's college education, take a nice vacation, or live comfortably in retirement. Examples of strategies people use to achieve well-thought-through personal financial goals include organizing their finances, investing to build their net worth, living within their means, saving for retirement, saving for a child's college tuition, minimizing taxes, protecting assets, and educating themselves about investments.

Money-management strategies such as these help people achieve their financial goals. And they will also help us create eternal wealth. That's because we don't bypass money-management strategies to create eternal wealth. We use them. And the better we get at effectively managing our money, the more capacity we have to create eternal wealth.

When our attention is focused on creating eternal wealth, it means we recognize that one day we are going to die. And when we die, we are going to account for the work we have done and Jesus is going to judge our work (Romans 14:10-12; Hebrews 10:30). In fact, Jesus is going to be the friend who welcomes us into eternal dwelling places, where we will do our accounting and he will do the judging (John 14:1-3). Therefore, when we're making plans for how we're going to use our money, it would be wise for us to include uses that will please Jesus. Using our money in ways that please Jesus is what Jesus meant when he said, "Use worldly wealth to make friends for yourself who will welcome you into eternal dwellings" (Luke 16:9).

The problem we run into is that we get good at doing the first part of Jesus' command (using worldly wealth) and fall slack on the latter part (making friends for yourself who will welcome you into eternal dwellings). We get too friendly with the worldly wealth itself and forget that the purpose for wealth is to gain friends (specifically Jesus) so we're welcomed into eternal dwellings. When we become too friendly with worldly wealth, it begins to use us instead of us using it.

The antidote that protects us from the fatal attraction to money and the things money can buy is giving. That is why paying tithes and giving generous offerings are critical components of our eternal-wealth-creating strategies. But when it comes to maintaining an appropriate detachment from our money and material possessions, giving money may not be the only thing God requires of us.

Letting Go of Cherished Things

In the months following God's speaking to me about pouring my love into my family, and his getting my negative response, he used a giving lesson to speak to me about my attachment to things.

I attended a women's prayer breakfast one Saturday morning and was greatly blessed by the speaker and her prophetic ministry to many of the women that day, including me. It had been eight months since that eventful day when God had redirected my priorities and yet I still hadn't obeyed. God used the speaker's prophetic ministry and the events of that morning to get my attention and to prepare me for the insecurity and fear I would face in only a few months when I suddenly quit my job.

The process began when he demonstrated his power and tenderness as he spoke to me through the prophet. Then something strange began to happen in that meeting. Women rose from their seats spontaneously, walked up to the speaker at the podium, and gave her pieces of jewelry—expensive jewelry made of gold, diamonds, and other precious stones. The speaker didn't ask for anything, and nobody called the women forward or announced the unexpected outpouring of generosity. It just happened, obviously prompted by the Holy Spirit.

I had never seen anything like it and I was stunned. *This is weird and absurd!* I thought. *These women have to be crazy to give away their valuable jewelry. Why are they doing it?* If they wanted to give the prophet a gift, why didn't they just give her cash or a check? Yet they kept streaming to the front, one by one, and laying their jewelry on the stage.

I looked down at the diamond tennis bracelet adorning my wrist. It was beautiful, expensive, and precious to me—a gift I had given myself on a trip to St. Thomas in the Virgin Islands. Then I froze as I heard God speak to my heart, "Give your bracelet to her."

"Oh no, not me!" I argued silently. "Not my tennis bracelet!"

God's response was firm and insistent: "Give it to her."

I knew then what was happening all around me. God was speaking to many women, directing them to give away pieces of jewelry. Perhaps they had resisted and argued too, but many of them were obeying him.

"Lord, I can write her a generous check," I countered, pouting to myself.

"I know you can, but I want you to give her the bracelet."

Slowly I unclasped the bracelet, took it to the front, and gave it away. I returned to my seat in great sorrow, and I drove home from the breakfast in tears. It was my first experience of being called by God to give sacrificially, the kind of giving that hurts. It was also a kind of giving that awakened my spirit to the reality of my pride, my connection to the things I owned, and my willingness (or lack thereof) to use my wealth to serve God by obeying him.

My husband and I had given away hundreds of thousands of dollars over our married life, but I had never given away something of personal and sentimental value. I would have gladly written a check for five thousand dollars. But the ache in my heart told me that the monetary value of the gift was not the issue. A big check would not have been a sacrifice at that time in my life, but giving away a bracelet to which I was connected emotionally was a big sacrifice.

My bracelet may have looked like just another expensive piece of jewelry to the women at that breakfast. But to me it was much more. It was a symbol of my success, accomplishment, station in society, and progress toward achieving the American Dream. Symbols of success that God allows us to gain and enjoy can be the hardest things to part with. We can become so "friendly" with them that they actually become idols for us, which is probably why God sometimes puts his finger on them and says, "Give it away." Your symbol may be the nice car you drive, your home, or the designer clothes and fur coat you wear. There is nothing intrinsically wrong with any of these nice things, but when they become cherished symbols of the good life to you, and when holding on to them is more important than giving them away in obedience to God, they can detour you from creating eternal wealth.

So, how do you respond to situations like the following?

- On the counter of the grocery store checkout line, you notice a container inviting customers to donate spare change toward finding a cure for a serious disease. The photo on the container portrays a sick child.
- In the weeks following a natural disaster that killed thousands, a number of charitable agencies broadcast the need for donations and volunteers for the massive relief effort. The death toll continues to mount.
- You learn that a single mom attending your Bible study group has been unemployed for several months. She is struggling to put food on the table, and her kids need shoes for school.
- The pastor announces a capital campaign to fund the construction of a much-needed education building for the church. He calls on congregation members to consider making a sacrificial pledge over the next three years.
- You hear about someone who needs reliable transportation. You sense God directing you to give away one of your cars, both of which are paid off—and he seems to be talking about the newer, nicer one.

You can't effectively execute your eternal-wealth-creating strategy in each such situation without loving God, loving your neighbor as yourself, and understanding the purpose of giving. Making the right choice begins with understanding that, from God's perspective, expressing love through giving is the means for creating eternal wealth.

Giving and the Creation of Eternal Wealth

In God's economic system, strategic financial management for creating eternal wealth must include giving. The world's economic system claims that, in order to create wealth, you must add to your resources, multiply, divide, and add again. God's principle is the opposite. In order to add to your wealth, you must first subtract. We must give in order to receive.

Jesus said the following:

> Give, and it will be given to you. A good measure, pressed down, shaken together and running over, will be poured into your lap. For with the measure you use, it will be measured to you. (Luke 6:38)

> Give to the one who asks you, and do not turn away from the one who wants to borrow from you. (Matthew 5:42)

> [To the rich man] If you want to be perfect, go, sell your possessions and give to the poor, and you will have treasure in heaven. Then come, follow me. (Matthew 19:21)

> It is more blessed to give than to receive. (Acts 20:35)

We are to view the giving commanded in the Bible as key in our financial-management strategy for creating eternal wealth. Giving demonstrates our willingness to invest our money, time, and material resources in the lives of people Jesus cares about. Giving is the manifestation of our desire to seek justice, love mercy, and walk humbly before God. It is a response of love for God and others, not a duty we must perform. Paul wrote, "If I give all I possess to the poor and surrender my body to the flames, but have not love, I gain nothing" (1 Corinthians 13:3). We should regard giving to God and others as a privilege and a joy. Paul said, "Each man should give what he has decided in his heart to give, not reluctantly or under compulsion, for God loves a cheerful giver" (2 Corinthians 9:7). As we generously and joyfully give when opportunities arise, we are creating a tangible return that can never be taken away. We are demonstrating our attachment to and friendship with Jesus. We are creating eternal wealth.

The reason it is more blessed to give than to receive is that the act of giving exercises our detachment from things and attachment to God. The more we detach from things by giving and attach to God, the greater our capacity to give becomes. As our capacity to give increases, so does the depth of our giving. And as the depth of our giving increases, the balance in our eternal wealth account also increases (Philippians 4:16-17). Plus, God will continually give back to us. The lyrics of a popular gospel song remind us that no matter how hard we might try, we can't beat God in giving.

Giving possessions is sometimes harder than giving money. When your financial wealth increases to a level of abundance where you have more than enough money, then giving money becomes easier to do, especially when you have a giving heart. But if God asks you to give away your possessions, those symbols of success, or the source of your wealth, then you'll really know how much you love and trust him.

The challenge the rich man faced had to do with giving away his symbols of success and giving up his status in the community. Jesus didn't ask him to give a substantial offering to the church. I'm sure, if he had, the rich man would have cheerfully given the offering since he certainly had the means to give it. Jesus asked the rich man to sell all his possessions, give the proceeds to the poor, and follow him. It would be like Jesus asking any successful businessperson today to sell her business, sell her home, sell her car, sell her boat, sell all her toys, and come follow him. Would you do it? When you can give away your possessions as an act of obedience to God, then you'll know you have detached from things, left Babylonian captivity, and entered into a place of freedom and eternal abundance in God's kingdom.

It's not easy, but we have to remove the label "mine" from our money and possessions. Does that sound like something you are ready to do?

Generosity Toward Others

The motive for giving varies from person to person and situation to situation. When we forget about our desire to "make friends with Jesus" and instead allow the invisible hand of self-interest to be our motivation for giving, then giving can actually be an act of control or manipulation. You'll give to get something back from the recipient or you'll give when you want a favor. The invisible hand of self-interest also causes people to give as a way of boosting their ego or compensating for low self-esteem. For example, you might give to the poor because it magnifies your prosperity in the eyes of others. You might publicly give large offerings to your church because it shows people how successful you are. You might refuse to receive from others because your low self-esteem can't be elevated if you're the recipient of the gift instead of the giver. You might give when you want attention from others and you might give when you need to feel important. Any reward or benefit received from giving motivated by the need to satisfy self-interest is immediate and temporal.

Generous giving motivated by love, compassion, and a pure heart, however, creates eternal wealth. When you give as an act of love and compassion, and from a pure desire to be generous toward others, you won't have an expectation of receiving anything from people. Jesus let us know that giving done with the expectation of getting something in return offers no hope of an eternal reward.

> Take heed that you do not do your charitable deeds before men, to be seen by them. Otherwise you have no reward from your Father in heaven. Therefore, when you do a charitable deed, do not sound a trumpet before you as the hypocrites do in the [church] and in the

streets, that they may have glory from men. Assuredly, I say to you, they have their reward. But when you do a charitable deed, do not let your left hand know what your right hand is doing, that your charitable deed may be in secret; and your Father who sees in secret will Himself reward you openly. (Matthew 6:1-4, NKJV)

What does this spirit of generosity look like in today's world? Here are a number of examples that have come to my attention.

A guitar-playing youth pastor at a summer camp gave his guitar to a student he didn't even know because he sensed God saying the girl needed it more than he did. This rather homely, "uncool" girl had asked if she could play the guitar during a break. She wasn't very good, but her face beamed with joy at the unexpected gift. And the youth pastor went home blessed by the opportunity to share his instrument at God's request.

One person I heard about puts a five-dollar bill in her pocket each day with this prayer: "Lord, show me someone who needs this money today." She has trained herself to be sensitive to the needs of others, from buying someone coffee at Starbucks to sharing with a homeless person on the street.

A Christian businessman and his wife felt their ministry was to make sure the pastors in their small town had reliable transportation. They were known to drive by the pastors' homes to look for tires that were worn and needing replacement. Then they would arrange to provide a new set of tires. They also bought good used cars for pastors in need. They had a modest income, but they found great joy in serving God by meeting pastors' needs.

A man I know was sitting in his car in the drive-through lane at a fast-food restaurant one lunchtime. Suddenly he was surprised by a thought that seemed to come from God: "Pay for the car behind you." He didn't know the person in the car behind him, and he didn't follow through on the idea. But the experience prompted him to ask God for a second chance to develop a generous spirit. Now he looks for opportunities to secretly buy meals for unsuspecting people at drive-through windows and in restaurants.

Generosity is contagious. I came across the story of an attendant in a parking garage near the University of Nebraska. The attendant said it is not unusual for drivers to pay the parking fee for the vehicles behind them, especially after sporting events at the university. It's a random act of kindness and generosity that makes people smile. But the following story, which occurred after a ballet at the campus performing arts center, surprised even the attendant.

> A man gave me double the fee and asked that I let the people in the next car know he'd paid for them too. "You're all set," I told the teenagers in the van. Then they paid for the next guy. The chain reached the tenth car. A new record!
>
> Car No. 11 pulled up: A mom driving an old station wagon. She'd won tickets and wanted her daughter to see her first ballet, but didn't have money for parking. I told her the car in front had already paid.
>
> "No kidding! I prayed God would help me with this." In this case, I guess it wasn't such a random act after all.[2]

A member of a local church anonymously gave $1 million to his church. The anonymous nature of the gift kept people from praising him for his generosity. Instead the members of the congregation praised God for his goodness. And the generous gift helped the church expand its ministry.

I think this is how you grow to become the cheerful giver mentioned in 2 Corinthians 9:7. The joy of generous giving doesn't come from other's knowing about it; it comes from doing it. Jesus said, "Give, and it will be given to you" (Luke 6:38). It's an investment principle. You can't earn any

Making Friends Who Will Welcome Us into Eternal Dwellings

Things to Remember
1. Christ has gone ahead into eternity, and he is the one who will receive us into eternal dwelling places.
2. We are not to trust money for our happiness, but we are to use it for our benefit as we pursue that which will make us happy: loving God.
3. We have a finite amount of time to use our substance for the benefit of God's kingdom.
4. Money invested in the lives of others is money invested in God's kingdom.
5. Self-centered, shortsighted uses of money can keep us from being welcomed into eternity.
6. We are to keep all our worldly possessions in a subservient position as we serve God. The purpose for money is to help us serve God and work out our salvation. We cannot serve two masters.

Things to Do
1. Focus attention on our financial picture by thinking strategically about money.
2. Take advantage of the financial tactics the world uses to make and manage money so we don't waste our resources.
3. Plan where our money will go.
4. Give something back by investing money in the lives of other people.
5. Don't be lazy. What we build with our substance should result in some type of improvement over what we were given to work with.

dividends until you invest some principal. In God's economy you won't reap the dividends of joy until you invest yourself in others through generous giving. But God's dividends always outweigh the investment: "Pressed down, shaken together and running over…poured into your lap" (verse 38).

Using Worldly Wealth to Make Friends

Throughout this book I've talked about two things: loving God and making money. These two things form the pathway to eternal wealth. That pathway is not a shortcut to financial prosperity or a get-rich-quick formula. Choosing to walk down that pathway is not going to get you out of poverty overnight or guarantee that you'll become the next Bill Gates. The principles for creating eternal wealth aren't a step-by-step program to instant wealth; they are, however, the key that will unlock the door leading to the power of God to create wealth and to live an abundant life.

God's power to create wealth is comprised of his favor and grace. But you will never tap into God's favor and grace to create wealth if you don't get into position. Making your money last forever is about getting into position. It's about seeking first to gain citizenship in and live in the kingdom of God. And once you get into position, you will be able to create wealth that will benefit you for eternity.

To get into position for creating eternal wealth, we should be diligent in designing a strategy for managing money that will benefit our eternal life. We should be as diligent and industrious in the use of money to benefit our eternal welfare as people in the world are at making money for their temporal benefit. The long-term goal of our financial strategy is to be welcomed by Christ into eternal dwellings. It is to hear the Lord say, "Well done, good and faithful servant. Welcome into the joy of your Master's kingdom!"

The church is the only institution that has the potential to birth an environment wherein people from differing socioeconomic backgrounds who share one powerful and crucial core belief can come together to begin to help one another prepare for the coming changes in our economic climate. If the church is going to respond to the question, "What are we to do about the problems of unequal distribution of resources, poverty, and injustice created by our world's economic system?" we must work together. When I make this claim, I'm not trying to be overly optimistic or naive by ignoring the problems of racism and sexism that exist in the church and that have historically separated believers from one another. I'm simply suggesting that if we want to be salt and light for a hurting world in a changing economic environment, we must work together.

This is why God wants us to be rich—rich in our understanding of who we are in his kingdom and the purpose he has given us for our resources, skills, and abilities. He has given us the power to prosper because it is through our prosperity that we can reach out and help someone else prosper. That is the work of God's enterprise.

Questions for Reflection and Discussion

1. Our ability to create eternal wealth is directly impacted by our ability to effectively manage financial resources. On a scale from 1 to 10 (1 meaning "not organized" and 10 meaning "extremely organized," how would you rate your current level of organization with regard to your personal finances?

2. Strategies and tactics that people use to organize their finances include the following:
    a. Set financial goals.

b. Maintain a filing system for bills, receipts, and other important financial documents.
c. Pay bills on time and on the same predetermined dates each month (e.g., the first and the fifteenth).
d. Reduce or eliminate debt.
e. Limit credit card charges to amounts you can afford to pay in full the next month.
f. Keep an eye on your credit report. (You can get your credit report free three times per year at www.Free3BureauCredit Report.com.)
g. Save at least 10 percent of take-home income. (Build an emergency fund representing from three to six months' worth of expenses.)
h. Save for children's college tuition.
i. Invest in a 401k, IRA, or other retirement account.
j. Maintain adequate amounts of life, medical, dental, home, and auto insurance.
k. Have a will.
l. Subscribe to and read at least one money-management magazine per month.
m. Reconcile your bank account monthly.
n. Pay quarterly estimated taxes (this is especially important if you're self-employed).
o. Use online banking and personal finance software (Quicken, MSN Money) to help you manage your finances.

Which of these strategies or tactics do you need to add to your money-management plan to improve your organization?

3. Creating eternal wealth happens when we give. In what ways do you sense God challenging you to take your giving to the next level?

"Though one may be overpowered,

two can defend themselves.

A cord of three strands

is not quickly broken"

(Ecclesiastes 4:12).

Chapter 12

BUILDING RELATIONSHIPS AND STRATEGIC ALLIANCES

Creating eternal wealth is not about us; it's all about God and, in particular, about taking good care of the resources he has entrusted to us. Eternal wealth thus is a consequence, not a goal. It is the consequence of an intimate relationship with God, a deep level of trust in his Word, character developed in the image of God, and understanding of purpose. Eternal wealth is also a consequence of effectively managing business and economic resources and being committed to using resources to fulfill our God-given purpose and advance God's economy in the world.

Just as there are multiple ingredients for making a cake, so there are many ingredients involved in creating eternal wealth. The last component of purposeful and profitable action for creating eternal wealth is building relationships and strategic alliances. In fact, forming relationships and partnering with others are the binding agents that bring all these ingredients together and stir us up to produce eternal wealth.

The word *relate* means "to establish or demonstrate a connection between two things." When things are related, they share a common origin, existence, purpose, or destiny. You can be related by blood or marriage, or you can be related by shared goals or beliefs. Relationships can be intimate or casual, romantic or platonic, business or personal. They can build us up, nurture us, and strengthen us, or they can tear us down, drain our energy, and weaken our resolve. Throughout our lives we enter into and exit from many different types of relationships. In addition to thinking and working like an entrepreneur and strategically managing financial resources, purposeful and profitable action involves building and sustaining relationships that help us create eternal wealth.

Partnering with people who share our vision for fulfilling the mission of God's enterprise is a type of relationship that supports our efforts to create eternal wealth. Partners cooperate with one another to achieve a specified objective and are accountable to each other for achieving goals. Partners must be able to relate to each other in a manner that facilitates their reaching their shared objective. Consequently, relationships are the basis upon which partnerships are formed.

The Power of Partnerships

One evening I was driving home alone after having spent the day at a friend's house when I heard the audible voice of God speak to me again. The last time this had happened it had changed my life dramatically. This time I knew better than to kick against anything God had to say, but what he said left me baffled. God said, "Make me a cake first." When these words interrupted my thoughts, they had a vague ring of familiarity to them, but I didn't immediately know why.

As I continued to drive, I began to repeat the words over and over again. *Make me a cake first. Make me a cake first.* What did it mean? Finally I had a fuzzy recollection of a story in the Old Testament that I thought might have those words in it.

When I got home, I went straight to my concordance and looked up a keyword so I could find the Scripture. There it was: 1 Kings 17:7-16, the story of Elijah and the widow. I read the entire chapter, trying to make sense of what God was saying to me. How does somebody make God a cake? And what does it mean to make a cake for God *first*?

In time I figured out what God was trying to tell me.

In the story of Elijah and the widow, God illustrates the power of kingdom partnerships. When the widow made the decision to satisfy Elijah's need by making him a cake before using what was left over to make a cake for herself and her son, she tapped into the power of kingdom partnerships that released God's supernatural provision for multiplication and increase. Her resources never dwindled, because she was willing to partner with Elijah by giving a portion of her resources to him before she consumed any herself. Today we have the same opportunity to participate in kingdom partnerships.

The thing that characterizes a kingdom partnership and distinguishes it from other types of partnerships is who gets the glory from the work. Kingdom partnerships are formed between people, but God always gets the glory for the work performed by the partners. But when we devote ourselves to work that is focused on God's glory, we also position ourselves, by faith, to be the recipients of his supernatural provision for the work we do.

Kingdom partnerships are alliances formed between men and women of God called to work full time in church ministry and men and women of God called to work full time in marketplace ministry. When we form alliances between church ministries and marketplace ministries, it is for the purpose of doing work that will glorify God and build his kingdom. I believe this is a way we "make God a cake."

For us as entrepreneurial managers and business owners who spend most of our working hours in the marketplace, the way we can "make God a cake" and benefit from his supernatural power for multiplication and increase is by partnering with people who spend most of their working hours in church ministry. Our role is to help church leaders accomplish God's objectives. By investing our skills, abilities, and financial resources in partnerships formed through alliances with apostles, prophets, evangelists, pastors, and teachers employed in full-time ministry, who are equipping people all over the world to live a life of faith in Jesus Christ, we are able to achieve shared objectives.

These partnerships form a means by which marketplace leaders can invest in the work of the church in God's kingdom. Our investment of our know-how and material and financial resources contributes to the work of the church, and that creates eternal wealth. These partnerships also provide a link between the church and the marketplace. And they are a means through which we can invest our resources today so that we will be welcomed into eternal dwellings. From the church leaders' perspective, these partnerships are the source of resources—in the form of finances, material supplies, and know-how—that support the minister's execution of his or her vision.

Such partnership starts with building a relationship with a church in our community. Now, I realize that going to church is not the only way we serve God. We serve God whenever we do his will, and that should happen every day, not just when we walk into a church building. However, if we want to make God a cake, we have to partner with him, and partnering with God's happens when we do his will by executing our soul plan and building relationships with other people who are doing his work.

Partnerships are strengthened when each partner understands his or her respective role. Revelation 11:15 says the kingdom of this world shall become "the kingdom of our Lord and of his Christ." We are assigned the prestigious task of taking the marketplace of this world back for God. Therefore, whenever we make the decision to submit our lives to God, obey his commands, and invest in ourselves and others so that we're able to experience success for the glory of God, we position ourselves to partake in an anointing that empowers us to dominate the marketplace in the area of our gifting. And when each of us dominates the marketplace in the area of our gifting, we collectively dominate the marketplace for the sake of Jesus. We are called to be priests and kings in the marketplace who create eternal wealth!

Apostles, prophets, evangelists, pastors, and teachers have a different role than we do. They are spiritual leaders, shepherds, and overseers for the body of Christ. They teach us, lead us by example, and guide us into greater levels of knowledge and understanding of God's Word. They are concerned with our spiritual and physical health, welfare, and safety. We are called to dominate the marketplace in our area of gifting, and they equip us spiritually and mentally to respond to that call.

It's important to choose your partnerships wisely, because who you allow to pastor you or feed you spiritually will have a direct impact upon your success in the marketplace, your success in creating eternal wealth, and indeed your success in all areas of life. Think of it this way. When the widow partnered with Elijah, she wisely submitted her future well-being into the hands of an anointed prophet of God. As a result, her investment in his life brought her life. If she had invested her last provisions in the life of someone who didn't have God's anointing, her investment would not have produced the same life-giving results. So it is with us today.

What are the benefits of our partnership?

We share a common goal.
The church is a team whose task is to spread the news of the kingdom of God throughout the world, and we're members of that team. We each have different workplaces, but we share a common goal: to establish the kingdom

of God on the earth. The Bible says one can put a thousand to flight and two can put ten thousand (Deuteronomy 32:30). When we partner, we multiply each other's effectiveness in carrying out our shared vision.

We have a storehouse to which we bring our tithes and offerings.
Partnering with our pastor gives us a way to channel giving into the body of Christ. It gives us a place to bring our tithes and offerings.

A word of caution. Giving tithes and offerings does not give us authority to tell the pastor what to do, no matter how significant our gifts nor what our level of influence in the marketplace. If you have a relationship with your pastor whereby he or she looks to you for wise, godly counsel, then respect that relationship; don't abuse it. (This area can also challenge some pastors who may be tempted to give preferential treatment to successful businesspeople as a way to secure large gifts for the church or win their loyalty. James 2:1 warns us that we are not to show partiality to people (NKJV).) Trying to manipulate the pastor by giving large offerings or withholding giving as a means to show discontent does not hurt the pastor; it hurts the partnership, and that in turn hurts you. When you hurt the partnership, then you hurt God's church, which doesn't bode well for your relationship with God. Remember, when we bring our tithes and offerings to the church, we are giving to God and not people.

We need each other.
Every priest and king needs a prophet. Prophetic words guide us, sustain us, nourish us, direct us, warn us, admonish us, humble us, exhort us, and encourage us. Who is your prophet? Who speaks prophetically into your life? Hopefully, the answer to this question is your pastor. And if it's not, I think it should be.

When God places us under the authority of a particular pastor, then in addition to preaching and teaching the Word of God, that person should also be a prophet in our lives. You'll know whether your pastor is also your prophet because, if he or she is, the messages the pastor preaches will speak directly to your life's situation.

On many occasions God has used my pastor to answer questions I've asked in prayer. My pastor didn't come to me one-on-one to answer the questions. He or she answered the questions through the sermon. The pastor didn't even know he or she was answering my questions; rather, the pastor was simply preaching God's Word by inspiration of the Holy Spirit.

Having the benefit of being under the spiritual authority of a pastor who is also a prophet is enormous.

Our pastors need us. Nobody can fulfill their purpose and execute God's vision for their lives alone, not even a pastor. When we ally ourselves with our pastors and serve them, as together we serve God, we provide the resource they need to fulfill the vision of the church they pastor. Partners always need each other.

Partners share the credit.

The beauty of working with others in ministry to achieve a desired goal or objective is that every member of the team gets to share in the accomplishments of the team. When pastors preach and teach the Word of God in a way that empowers us to do great exploits for the kingdom of God in the marketplace, we win and the pastor wins. When we give our time and resources to God's church and support its mission, we win and the pastor wins. When we support evangelists or missionaries, then when they lead people into the kingdom of God, we all win. Each of us gets to share in the benefits and the credit that is being added to our accounts because of our good stewardship of God's resources and the fulfillment of his plan.

How does this work?

The best example I can give you of how kingdom partnerships benefit everyone involved comes from the partnerships I see at my church, The

City Church in Kirkland, Washington. It starts with the prophetic pastoral leadership of Dr. Wendell Smith. Pastor Wendell's preaching showed me how God has given us all gifts and how we have a responsibility to use those gifts to benefit his kingdom. It taught me that God is interested in our prosperity. And it revealed to me that when we are faithful in using our gifts as stewards of God's resources, he will open up the windows of heaven and cause us to prosper in every area of our life.

And Pastor Wendell's teaching didn't impact just my life. Every member of the church was exposed to this same fresh revelation. As we were taught how to use our money to bless God by blessing others, businesspeople throughout the church began to prosper in supernatural ways. And the level of giving at the church soared. I know. I used to be the church's chief financial officer. The church's budget is significant, and the ministries we are able to carry out are equally significant.

As the giving increased, so did the success stories. One businessperson in the real estate development industry experienced growth in excess of 100 percent during the 2003–04 recession because he refused to listen to the negative reports about our nation's economy and instead decided to trust in God's economy. Another person tells the story of how his business grew 1,300 percent in one year as a result of his learning how to make God a cake first. As a result of his business's supernatural growth, his giving increased to levels greater than he and his wife could have ever imagined. Another business owner tells a story of how he was able to grow his business without needing to do any self-marketing because God caused new clients to come to him. In effect, God promoted his business instead of him having to promote his business.

Then there's the story of the IRS claim against a certain business owner stating his business owed back taxes approaching one hundred thousand dollars due to errors made in tax filings. You know how difficult it is to prove the IRS wrong. But that is exactly what happened, and instead of the business owing the IRS, the IRS sent the business a refund.

Making God a cake first begins when we know our God-given purpose and the purpose for our prosperity. It begins with the development of a prosperous soul, and that doesn't happen without hearing the Word of God. It begins when we make the decision to use our gifts to benefit God's kingdom by fulfilling our soul plan. Our pastor's role is to teach us the truth about money and equip us to live free from Babylonian captivity. When that happens, we can respond by assuming our responsibility to give to God what we've been given before we consume it on ourselves. We can focus our marketplace exploits on the execution of our God-given soul plan. And we can partner with our pastor and other church leaders to expand the reach and influence of God's kingdom in the earth. That's how we make God a cake first. Everybody wins: ministers of the gospels, entrepreneurial managers and business owners, and most of all, God's kingdom.

And that's what it means to create eternal wealth.

Eternal Wealth Comes When We Make God a Cake First

On that pleasant summer evening when God told me to make him a cake first, he presented to me the key to financial prosperity with benefits that will last forever. Putting God first, dedicating our life to him, and partnering with like-minded people who want to do the will of God always leads to prosperity. God gets all the glory when we run that race.

The race we're assigned to run in life will take us through many twists and turns, uphill and downhill, and through cloudy days and stormy nights. But that race will always have the same destination: the prize of our high calling in Christ Jesus. Pursuing our high calling in Christ starts by putting God first. And when we put God first, he gets the glory.

When we understand the purpose for our life and prosperity, the marketplace represents a wonderful place of opportunity for us to pursue our high calling in Christ Jesus. God is ready and willing to help us realize our full potential in the marketplace. He is ready and willing to help us manage material and financial resources. God wants us to discover our purpose, develop our skills and abilities, and then use those gifts to make a difference in the world.

It is possible to prosper financially while living a life of obedience to God because obedience to him always puts us in the right race, and when we run the right race, God will equip us to win. Running the race leads us to our soul plan—the plan for the use of our gifts that will meet the needs of others. Pursuing our soul plan keeps us from developing self-centered attitudes and objectives, and it also keeps our success dependent upon our relationship with God. Giving is the key to our financial prosperity.

When we devote our work life to making God a cake first, we avoid the traps that lead to Babylonian captivity. These traps of greed, selfishness, and disobedience to God are set by our adversary, who wants us to forfeit running God's race for the sake of running the world's race. Running the world's race may give us financial benefits today, but those benefits are only temporal. Why not go for the eternal benefits of prosperity that are reserved for those who do the will of God?

Following the stewardship principles for creating eternal wealth, developing a prosperous soul, discovering our purpose, and engaging in purposeful and profitable action guards our heart from trying to love God while serving money. Creating eternal wealth frees us from the guilt that is so often associated with being a successful, financially prosperous person in God's kingdom. Executing our soul plan gives us an opportunity to influence the lives of people we work with and build the marketplace of God's kingdom. Our influence can reach so far as to include sharing the gospel of Jesus Christ with friends we make in the workplace. Executing our soul plan coupled with partnering with ministers of the gospel answers the question of how our desire to be successful in the marketplace fits in with the Great Commission. It gives our work meaning beyond the fulfillment of a job or career, and it expands the scope of our reach to work performed by others called to full-time ministry. It gives us a reason to make money.

Understanding our role and responsibilities and the role and responsibilities of our ministry partners abates feelings of inferiority. Each person has an important part to play in the execution of God's plan for salvation in his kingdom. Understanding our role generates vision and passion that increase our sense of value to God's kingdom.

Making God a cake first happens when we build partnerships, starting with our relationship with God, that enable us to put our substance in his hands and do work for which he gets the glory. The quantity of our substance, whether large or small, isn't important. What is important is our understanding that, when we seek intimacy with God and partner with each other, God can do more with the first portion we devote to him than we can do with the whole amount we refuse to give to him. And when God multiplies and increases our substance, he always gets the glory!

It's Sunday morning. Congregations gather to fellowship with one another and worship God. Praise and worship teams, choirs, and musicians lead congregations in songs celebrating God's goodness. The preacher preaches a message of encouragement and hope. People confess their sins and seek God's forgiveness. Newcomers hear the gospel message, experience the love and fellowship of the congregation, and put their faith in Jesus Christ.

Then comes offering time, that point in the service when men and women, entrepreneurial managers and business owners, pastors and ministers of the gospel, bring to God's altar a portion of their financial resources.

This portion reflects the results of their good stewardship. It is a testimony of their faithfulness and God's goodness. It's the tangible representation of the glory of God at work in their lives. They give generously because God has been generous to them. As the plate is passed, amid shouts of joy or in silent reverence, the process that keeps the wheels turning in God's economy goes forward. One by one, wise people in God's kingdom use money to make friends for themselves—friends with the King of kings and the Lord of lords. And because of their faithfulness, one day they will hear the words "Well done, my good and faithful servant. You have been faithful with a little. Come, now I will give you true riches and make you ruler over much. Enter into the joy of your Master's eternal kingdom."

Notes

Introduction

1. The author believes that God is neither male nor female. The use of the masculine pronoun in reference to God is for the purposes of simplification only and should not be construed to imply that God is male.

Chapter 1

1. Luisa Kroll and Allison Fass, "The World's Billionaires," Forbes.com, March 8, 2007, accessed online at http://www.forbes.com/billionaires/2007/03/07/billionaires-worlds-richest_07billionaires_cz_lk_af_0308billie_land.html.
2. Myles Munroe, *The Burden of Freedom* (Lake Mary, FL: Creation House, 2000), 240.

Chapter 4

1. Quoted in Malcolm Muggeridge, *Something Beautiful for God* (New York: Harper & Row, 1971), 74.
2. Adapted from Ptolemy Tompkins, "Shoe Shine," *Guideposts*, June 2005, 24–26; and from Lee Cowan, "Hospital Has a Shoeshine Saint," CBSNews.com, January 14, 2005, accessed online at http://www.cbsnews.com/stories/2005/01/14/eveningnews/main667174.shtml?source=search_story.

Chapter 6

1. Adam Smith, *The Wealth of Nations*, chap. 2, accessed online at http://www.bibliomania.com/2/1/65/112/frameset.html.

Chapter 7

1. Margaret Parkin, *Tales for Coaching* (London: Kogan Page, 2001), 77.

Chapter 8

1. Frank Main and Natasha Korecki, "The Welfare-Fraud Link," *Chicago Sun-Times*, April 9, 2006, accessed online at http://www.amren.com/mtnews/archives/2006/04/the_welfarefrau.php.
2. "Defrauding Medicare and Medicaid with Ease," National Center for Policy Analysis, accessed online at http://www.ncpa.org/health/pdh5.html.
3. Barbara Ley Tofler and Jennifer Reingold, *Final Accounting: Ambition, Greed, and the Fall of Arthur Andersen* (New York: Random House, 2004), excerpt accessed online at http://www.randomhouse.com/acmart/catalog/display.pperl?isbn=9780767913836&view=excerpt.
4. Gene Klann, *Building Character: Strengthening the Heart of Good Leadership* (New York: Wiley, 2007), 35.
5. Esther Wachs Book, *Why the Best Man for the Job Is a Woman* (New York: HarperBusiness, 2000), 12.
6. Ibid., 27-28.
7. Robert T. Kiyosaki, *Rich Dad's Cashflow Quadrant* (New York: Warner, 1998), 34.

Chapter 9

1. "All God's Chillun Got Wings," Negro Spirituals, accessed online at http://www.negrospirituals.com/news-song/all_god_s_chillun_got_wings.htm.
2. Tony Pugh, "U.S. Economy Leaving Record Numbers in Severe Poverty," February 22, 2007, McClatchy Washington Bureau, accessed online at http://www.realcities.com/mld/krwashington/16760690.htm.
3. Amy K. Glasmeier, "Tax Policy at the Heart of Rising Income Inequality in the U.S.," Penn State Poverty in America, November 6, 2006, accessed online at http://www.povertyinamerica.psu.edu/.
4. Ibid.

5. Steven Greenhouse, "Borrowers We Be," NYTimes.com, September 3, 2006, accessed online at http://www.nytimes.com.
6. David H. Autor, Lawrence F. Katz, and Melissa S. Kearney, "Trends in U.S. Wage Inequality: Re-Assessing the Revisionists," NBER working paper 11627, September 2005, 32.

Chapter 10

1. Michael Gerber, *E-Myth Mastery* (New York: HarperCollins, 2005), xxxii.
2. Pino Audia and Chris Rider, "Entrepreneurs As Organizational Products Revisited," accessed online at http://www.haas.berkeley.edu/faculty/papers/audia_entrepreneurs_as_org_products.pdf.
3. Bill Hewlett and David Packard both graduated from Stanford. Michael Dell, whose father is an orthodontist and mother is a money manager, dropped out of college at the University of Texas to start his company. No doubt his well-to-do family background, coupled with his formal education, contributed to his business success.
4. Marty Bates and others, "How Fast Is Too Fast?" *McKinsey Quarterly* 3 (2001): 1.
5. Carl J. Schramm, *The Entrepreneurial Imperative* (New York: HarperCollins, 2006), 3.

Chapter 11

1. Arthur A. Thompson Jr. and A. J. Strickland III, *Strategic Management: Concepts and Cases,* 4th ed. (Plano, TX: Business Publications, 1987), 7.
2. Jodi Panko, "Pass It On: End of the Line," *Guideposts,* July 2005, 20–21.

Recommended Reading

Collins, Jim. *Good to Great.* New York: HarperCollins, 2001.
Gerber, Michael E. *E-Myth Mastery: The Seven Essential Disciplines for Building a World-Class Company.* New York: HarperCollins, 2005.
Kiyosaki, Robert T. *Rich Dad, Poor Dad.* New York: Warner Books, 1997.
———. *Rich Dad's Cashflow Quadrant.* New York: Warner Books, 1998.
Munroe, Myles. *The Burden of Freedom.* Lake Mary, FL: Creation House, 2000.
Schramm, Carl J. *The Entrepreneurial Imperative: How America's Economic Miracle Will Reshape the World (and Change Your Life).* New York: HarperCollins, 2006.
Welch, Jack. *Winning.* New York: HarperCollins, 2005.

About the Author

JULAINE SMITH is a successful certified public accountant with more than 16 years experience in corporate finance. She has managed numerous mergers and acquisitions and helped raise $700 million in an initial public offering. Smith reached the top of her corporate career as division vice-president of finance and chief financial officer at AT&T Broadband. However, Smith came to the realization in 2001 that financial success was not the panacea. She needed to create a lifestyle in which her relationship with her family, her relationship with God, and her career pursuits were in sync with her ultimate ideals and desire to glorify God. Responding to God's call on her life, Smith integrated more than a decade of corporate finance experience with sound biblical doctrine and developed a framework for prosperity in God's economy. In 2005, after taking a four-year sabbatical from her corporate finance career, Smith founded ARISE Business Solutions, a business development firm whose mission is to equip entrepreneurs for business success through teaching centered on the 7 Eternal Wealth Principles and through services focused on developing financial management and leadership skills. Smith is also the former chief financial officer for The City Church, Kirkland, WA. She completed her public accounting experience at Price Waterhouse and received her Bachelor of Science degree in Business Administration–Accounting from California State University–Hayward.

She has been married to Terence for twenty-six years, and they have one son, Jonathan, age eighteen. The Smiths reside in Bellevue, Washington.